ASSET MANAGEMENT HANDBOOK FOR REAL ESTATE PORTFOLIOS

ASSET MANAGEMENT HANDBOOK FOR REAL ESTATE PORTFOLIOS

6/1/2013 (Version 5.0)

R. M. Santucci

Library of Congress Control Number:		2013914464
ISBN:	Hardcover	978-1-4836-8287-7
	Softcover	978-1-4836-8286-0
	Ebook	978-1-4836-8288-4

Rev. date: 10/08/2013

To order additional copies of this book, contact:
Xlibris LLC
1-888-795-4274
www.Xlibris.com
Orders@Xlibris.com
110494

Table of Contents

ASSET MANAGEMENT HANDBOOK
Copyrighted Material

The Asset Management Handbook contains copyrighted material parts of which are being made available in free PDF documents as a public service. Any reuse without express permission is prohibited including but not limited to the following:

1. **Resale**. The Asset Management Handbook, whether in whole or part, may not be reproduced and sold in any format, including print, digital, electronic file, fax or other medium.

2. **Publication of Data**. The Asset Management Handbook, whether in whole or part, may not be distributed or published in any format, including print, digital, electronic file, fax or other medium without obtain express permission.

3. **Applications/Software**. The Asset Management Handbook, whether in whole or part, may not be incorporated for use in any kind of computer—or Web-based application, calculator, database or other automated, electronic or digital device, instrument or software except as licensed by Urban Renovation Consultants, Inc.

Excerpting Asset Management Handbook Data

Excerpts of Asset Management Handbook may not take the form of a chart or table that simulates the manner in which the data is displayed. Excerpts of Asset Management Handbook data may, however, be made as part of a narrative, provided that the sum total of all excerpts from any publisher in all formats does not exceed data from more than 10 pages.

Citation Guidelines

When excerpting Asset Management Handbook data, refer to the "Asset Management Handbook" as in the following examples:

" . . . according to the Asset Management Handbook . . . ."

" . . . as compiled in the Asset Management Handbook . . . ."

All excerpts must be accompanied by one or more instances of the following acknowledgements of copyright:

"© 2013 Urban Renovation Consultants, Inc. Complete text from the Asset Management Handbook can be purchased by request from *urcusa@ mac.com.*

Licensing of 2013 Asset Management Handbook Data

For permission to license data from the 2013 Asset Management Handbook for use in any kind of computer—or Web-based application, calculator, database or other automated, electronic or digital device, instrument or software, send a request via email to *urcusa@mac.com* and include the following:

- a description of the application, calculator or device for which use of the data is being requested. Include the length of time for which the license is sought.
- a detailed description of the material to be licensed (e.g. specific projects, cities, etc.).

SELECTED TITLES BY
R.M. SANTUCCI

Substantial Rehabilitation / New Construction, Van Nostrand, New York, N.Y., Editor, 1991

Multifamily Selective Rehabilitation, Van Nostrand, New York, N.Y., Editor, 1991

A Consumer's Guide to Home Improvement, Renovation & Repair—John Wiley & Sons, Inc. New York, N.Y., Primary author, 1995, A Book of the Month Club alternative selection

Business Planning for Affordable Housing Developers, Author, Xlibris 2013

Residential Green Building NeighborWorks America, Author, 2005

Texts and Workshop—*27 Topics Available Including . . .*

Housing Production Management: The Essential Subsystems

Value Engineering in Housing Development

The Efficient Developer: Best Practices

The Property & Asset Management Practicum—A 5 Session Intervention

Cost Reduction in Property Management

Advanced Green Building Techniques

Building Healthy Homes

Creating the Accessible Home—Universal Design

Capital Reserves Overview: Keeping Buildings Operating

ACKNOWLEDGEMENTS

There are always a myriad of people, personalities, and situations that create the path of knowledge and experience that their sharing.

David Fromm was my earliest mentor, a gentleman whom I've known for ages since his times in Pennsylvania and Chattanooga. I remember the first time he explained what an asset manager was. He is one of the prime movers in the affordable asset management field and deserves serious recognition for his extensive contributions.

Michael Wiencek, an outstanding architect. On my fourth multifamily rehabilitation in 1987 he was forced to calculate a partial deposit to a replacement reserve for a 50-unit building. I became empowered knowing that traditional rules of thumb were not only not accurate, but self-delusional.

Roger Lewis. Not often enough does a training facilitator run across an extraordinary participant from whom lessons are learned as Plato learned from Aristotle, I learned tremendously from a young engineer who builds spreadsheets twice as complicated as mine and explains them to his maintenance personnel with a clarity that I can only wish for.

Michael Barber. In designing and delivering my 5-week asset management practicum, no one was more demanding of objectives, outcomes and appropriate adult training than Michael. He crafted the multi-media, multi-session delivery for the New Jersey nonprofit association.

My many sponsors. Each time I work with a group of six to ten portfolio asset managers, I learn a ton. This is possible due to the significant support of national sponsors. They include: The Enterprise Foundation, now Enterprise Community Partners; LISC, especially their Connecticut office; the Impact Capital in Washington State, especially the Denver office; Fort Worth Foundation and the consortia in Alabama.

Virginia my asset manager. She saw deeply hidden value in a young carpenter. She now has asset management nightmares that 10 heat pumps in her rental homes will all fail on the same 102 degree summer 4th of July weekend.

Beth Lindow spends many hours of tedious writing, rewriting, editing, then putting up with me changing my mind to create 1000s of pages of manuscripts.

Shawn Kaltenberg deals directly with our publishers and keeps things working while I wander around the world helping housing providers today.

Chris Roelofs is our illustrator and his whimsical but technically correct art enlivens a very boring subject.

To Steve Smith of AHC, the earliest of my partners in crime: Steve's acumen in the financial and regulatory field was a key to my property development success. Without his keen eye for regulatory compliance, I might have easily led our nascent nonprofit into a swamp that neither one of us could exit.

My Participants. Over the years, I have worked with some of the most gifted and effective real estate developers in the affordable housing business. During Asset Management Practicums, I visit the sites of the case studies to mentor the primary writer of the asset management plan. Each encounter offers: policies, procedures, tools and attitudes that are effective and useful to future participants. Thank you for sharing and allowing me to pass on your techniques to the entire industry.

HISTORIC VIEW OF ASSET MANAGEMENT

THE GOLDEN GOOSE

Even though the golden goose gets a flying start, the "archer" of every rising cost eventually takes it down. It is true in the castles of Europe and the peasants' homes that surrounded them. It is not whether the archer will take down the golden goose, it is when and with how much force.

HOW TO USE THIS BOOK

All of URC's written products are pragmatic, do-it-yourself directions to help practitioners in their day-to-day work. This manual is devised to integrate with a Workbook that can be downloaded from the book's website—www.assetmanagement.com The Workbook is also an attachment to a very large Excel spreadsheet that is preloaded with Capital Needs Assessment components in 5 different areas.

Overview

We start with an academic overview of the roles of the asset manager. It took me 2 years to figure the relationship out. We review "real" examples of asset management plans where the identity of the individual properties have been masked. They are real reports on real properties at different stages.

Your Case Study

The best way to internalize the ideas presented is to pick a property and run it through the various inspections, analyses, measurements and see how it works for you. Experimenting with various policies and procedures will help inform your decision to complete the report in-house or with your new understanding of the requirements, you will be preparing an RFQ for outside personnel.

Asset Management Reports

In the long run, no matter who does the technical evaluations of the property, the property owner is responsible to document and monitor the health of the properties. It is not productive to wait until the property is in danger of foreclosure to worry about its physical condition.

This pragmatic book will walk you through these areas. We help you fill in the narrative and Excel spreadsheet so that your properties stay healthy well into the next century.

Chapter 1

ASSET MANAGEMENT HANDBOOK

INTRODUCTION TO ASSET MANAGEMENT ISSUES

Theme: It's all ok, until we run out of money.

Learning Objectives: • To examine materials and book layout

                                • To review Capital Reserve issues

                                • To identify Asset Management roles

                                • To identify Property Management roles

Essential Vocabulary: — Replacement Reserves
                                — Syndication
                                — Capital Needs Assessment
                                — Asset Management
                                — Project Reserves
                                — Replacement Reserve Policy
                                — Home Written Agreements

DCR Out ECR In

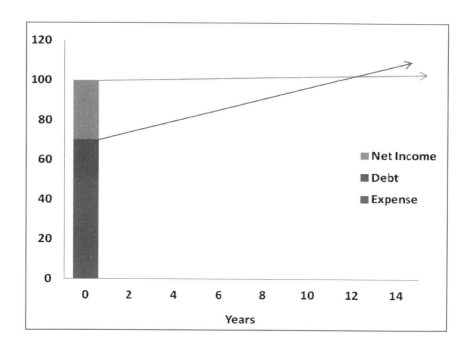

Opening Expenses Always Catch Surplus Income

All proformas assume that expenses inflate at a higher rate than income. Eventually this causes the property to first break even and then begin to lose ever increasing amounts of money from operating losses. Financial institutions like to plot this crossover point to assure that it is well after their funds have been repaid. For an owner assuming 50 to 100 year ownership, the crossover point merely marks a milestone in the life cycle that identifies the need to refinance or recapitalize the property.

DCR vs ECR

DCR is Debt Coverage Ratio. It is net operating income divided by debt service. Expense Coverage Ratio (ECR) examines the entire gambit of expenses versus the net income. In properties with very little debt, the DCR offers a false sense of long-term security.

THE OVERVIEW OF ASSET MANAGEMENT CHALLENGES
FINANCIAL CONDITION OF 26 DEVELOPMENTS

A key way to assess risk is to analyze the annual financial audits of the developments owned by the nonprofits. The financial analysis examines five indicators of the financial health of sampled developments: (1) reserves; (2) asset/liability balances; (3) current assets and accounts receivable; (4) balance of revenues versus expenses; and (5) use of nonrecurring funds for operating costs. Three of the most critical risks found in this group were . . . .

Insufficient Reserves

Capital reserves are funds set aside for repairs and improvements to the property that are too extensive to include in the operating budget. Operating reserves are monies set aside to cover unanticipated increases in operating expenses or shortfalls in income.

The properties examined in this study display a problematic pattern in both capital and operating reserve balances. Only 6 of 23 developments (26 percent) had capital reserves of more than 2 percent of the replacement value of the property, a commonly used industry minimum. Of the 23, 5 had no capital reserves whatsoever. Given the importance of capital reserves, it is safe to say that 17 of the 23 developments examined (those with reserves less than 2 percent) are in a dangerous position.

On the operating reserve side, the picture is even worse. Fourteen of the 23 reporting developments (61 percent) had no operating reserves at all. Another 4 had operating reserves of less than 10 percent of their operating budget. Only 3 developments reported reserves over 20 percent of operating costs, the number that the U.S. Department of Housing and Urban Development (HUD) considers the minimum for public housing authorities.

Imbalance of Revenues Versus Expenses

Of all the indications of management performance that can be drawn from annual audits, the revenues/expense balance is perhaps the most relevant. Regardless of any other financial difficulties a housing development has, a repeated practice of spending more money than is taken in will quickly produce devastating results.

The last year's audits reveal that among the developments in our sample, 15 out of 28 were spending more than they were taking in. And the overspending was serious. For 11 of these 15 developments, the deficit was more than 10 percent of annual operating expenditures, for 10 properties it was over 20 percent, and for 7 it was over 30 percent. The owners of these properties are dealing with the issue by allowing their accounts payable to rise to a dangerous level, or by using nonrecurring income (such as tax credit payments or foundation grants) to balance the budget. Neither solution is acceptable.

Several factors contribute to operating deficits. Expenses typically exceed revenues at developments where rent collections fall short of 95 percent of the rent roll. However, rent collection is not a problem at about half of the sampled properties that are operating "in the red." In these cases, the problem of negative cash flow most often stems from higher-than-anticipated costs and/or short-sighted underwriting.

Subsidizing Operating Costs with Other Income

When income is not sufficient to cover operating costs, property owners commonly tap other sources to pay bills. The problem is that the vast majority of those other sources, such as tax credit payments, insurance settlements, foundation grants, loans, and increases in the level of accounts payable, are not consistently available.

Of the 28 properties reporting, 14 relied on one or more source of nonrecurring funds. Within a period of a year or two most of these developments will have to find some other sources of funds to balance their budgets. They may or may not be successful, and constant fund-raising efforts take precious time away from other critical management tasks.

Low Quality of Rehabilitation/New Construction

Half of the 34 developments covered in the fieldwork faced management difficulties whose origins were in the quality of their rehabilitation or construction. We found two major reasons for inadequate rehabilitation or new construction:

1) Inadequate construction budgets. The buildings are brought "on line" without a reasonable level of rehabilitation. As a result, management inherits the problems created by the work that was cut from the budget or performed at lowest cost. We found these problems in developments in all six cities. Construction budgets may be inadequate for at least two major reasons. First, the nonprofit often underestimates costs, either through errors of judgment or because it lacks adequate information on the condition of the property to support accurate cost projections. Second, the nonprofit may undertake rehabilitation or new construction despite an awareness that the budget is inadequate because it has other important reasons for doing the project. e.g., to save a building that is at risk, to renovate a property that is strategically important to the neighborhood, or to accommodate funders who are eager to see a project move forward.

2) Poor workmanship and dishonesty among contractors.

In general, we found that nonprofits are working hard through their management efforts to overcome problems resulting from inadequate or poor work in the construction phase. But often, there are considerable costs involved in rectifying inherited physical deficiencies.

Adopted From: *Confronting the Management Challenge* by Community Development Research Center

ASSET MANAGEMENT & PROPERTY MANAGEMENT ROLES

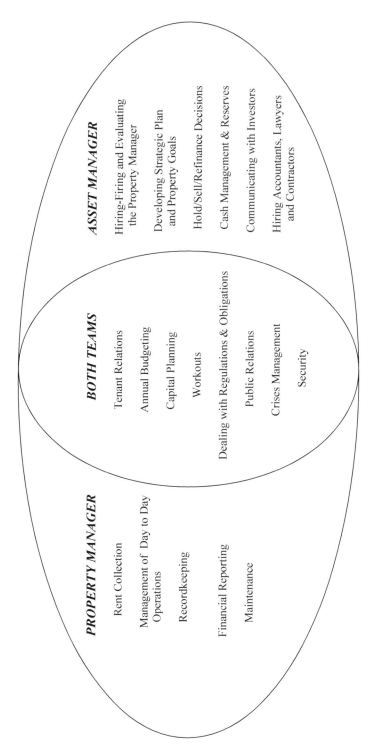

PROPERTY MANAGER

Rent Collection

Management of Day to Day Operations

Recordkeeping

Financial Reporting

Maintenance

BOTH TEAMS

Tenant Relations

Annual Budgeting

Capital Planning

Workouts

Dealing with Regulations & Obligations

Public Relations

Crises Management

Security

ASSET MANAGER

Hiring-Firing and Evaluating the Property Manager

Developing Strategic Plan and Property Goals

Hold/Sell/Refinance Decisions

Cash Management & Reserves

Communicating with Investors

Hiring Accountants, Lawyers and Contractors

What are the Specific Functions of Your Asset Management?

WHAT ARE THE SPECIFIC FUNCTIONS OF ASSET MANAGEMENT?

Asset management and property management functions overlap in roles while also maintaining autonomy. Practioners identified 3 types of roles: 1) functions that are exclusive to asset management, 2) functions that are exclusive to property management, and 3) areas of overlap between asset management and property management. The following summarized the relationships of those functions:

Asset Management Functions
   A.   Oversight of the Property Manager
   B.   Development of Strategic Plan and Property Goals
   C.   Hold/Sell/Refinance Decisions
   D.   Cash Management and Reserves
   E.   Communicating with Investors
   F.   Hiring Accountants, Lawyers and Contractors

Property Management Functions (Not covered in this manual)
   G.   Rent Collection
   H.   Management of Day-to-Day Operations
   I.   Record Keeping
   J.   Financial Reporting
   K.   Maintenance

Overlapping Functions
   L.   Security
   M.   Tenant Relations
   N.   Annual Budgeting
   O.   Capital Planning
   P.   Workouts
   Q.   Addressing with Regulatory Obligations
   R.   Public Relations
   S.   Disaster Response

50 QUESTIONS TO DEFINE YOUR
ASSET MANAGEMENT POLICY

A. Oversight of Property Manager

A key role of the Asset Management function is to oversee and supervise the property manager to champion the long-term interests of the property. The property manager must focus on day-to-day operation of the property including rent collection and routine maintenance. Asset management practices require persistent analysis of the information generated by the property manager with an eye toward the long-term horizon. Questions to think about include:

1. What information must a property manager provide?
2. How to hold the property manager accountable?
3. What benchmarks to use?
4. How to maintain proactive property management?
5. How costs can be minimized and revenues maximized?
6. Is the property manager meeting all regulatory and reporting requirements?

(See Attachment 2-1 Home Provisions Required Clauses)

B. Development of Strategic Plan and Property Goals

Asset Management oversees and directs long-term planning for a property according to the goals of the owner. Questions relating to long-term planning include:

1. What are our long-term goals for the property?
2. What is the required cash flow stream from the property?
3. Can the building cover the owner's social service and asset management costs?
4. How would external events such as changes in public policy or the loss of subsidies influence the property goals?
5. What are the tax consequences of ownership?

C. Hold/Sell/Refinance Decisions

The asset manager tracks debt obligations and decides whether to hold, refinance or sell a particular property. Questions relating to refinancing, sales, and dispositions include:

1. Have interest rates declined substantially since the property was last financed?
2. What opportunities have arisen that could reduce carrying costs?
3. How do subsidy restrictions impact refinancing, sales and disposition options?
4. Under what conditions will disposition be considered/required?
5. Do the benefits to the organization and community justify the resources and costs associated with continuing ownership?

D. Cash Management and Reserves

The asset manager must monitor cash flow, operating reserves, and capital replacement reserves. Questions relating to cash management and reserves include:

1. What constitutes "sufficient funds" in the reserve account?
2. How does the actual cash flow compare with proforma projections?
3. What performance measures forecast the financial condition?
4. What type of policy directives control and manage cash flow?
5. How are reserve funds and other earnings invested?
6. What are the anticipated capital needs for the property over the next 3 years?

E. Communicating with Investors

The asset manager is responsible for ensuring that investors and stakeholders receive accurate and timely information. The activities of the general partner or owner that materially affect the value or financial condition of the asset must be communicated. Questions relating to investor relations include:

1. How often should investors receive Profit and Loss Statements, Capital Expense Reports, Operating Expense Reports, Delinquency Reports and Rent Rolls?
2. What other information should be made available to investors?
3. How can the process be streamlined?

F. Hiring Accountants, Lawyers and Contractors

Numerous professional disciplines are involved in the ongoing operation of real estate. Asset Management is responsible for hiring and overseeing the works of such third-parry professionals. Questions relating to the hiring of third-party professionals include:

1. What services will be performed in-house vs contracted?
2. How are third-party professionals selected and hired?
3. Who oversees the work of third-party professionals?

OVERLAPPING FUNCTIONS

A. Tenant Relations

Asset Management and property management together establish policies both fair to tenants and serving the long-term interests of the owner. It is also critical that these policies are enforced adequately and fairly. Policies include tenant selection procedures, evictions, operating procedures, and security. Policy-related questions that include:

1. What key policies impact the long-term viability of a property?
2. Are there policy conflicts between one's mission as an affordable housing provider and one's mission as an asset manager?
3. How might such conflicts be resolved?
4. How do tenants have input in determining building policies?

B. Budgeting

Both the Asset Manager and property manager oversee the preparation of the annual budget and review the budget against actual expenses. Questions relating to annual planning include:

1. What are the financial goals for the building over the next year?
2. How has the property performed relative to previous years?
3. What preventative maintenance is needed?
4. What third party contracts require renewal?
5. Is there a need for any changes in policy?

C. Capital Planning

The long-term viability of a property requires careful attention to capital needs. A key joint asset management/property management responsibility is to update capital needs analyses and to undertake capital improvement programs. Questions that might be addressed in connection with capital needs, include:

1. How does an owner conduct long-term capital planning?
2. How are such expenses budgeted and financed?
3. What expenses are classified as capital expenses versus maintenance?
4. When must we refinance?

D. Workouts

In the event of a workout, Asset Management must work closely with the property manager as well as with all other parties to the transaction to resolve financial difficulties. Key workout questions include:

1. What are causes of the failure?
2. Can income be increased?
3. Can expenses be reduced?
4. Can negotiation with lenders and investors solve the issue?

E. Addressing Regulatory Obligations

Asset Management and Property Management must jointly deal with the myriad of federal, state and local statutory regulations and obligations to which they are subject. Key questions include:

1. Who drafts the monitoring plan?
2. What oversight is necessary to assure compliance?
3. Are specialized professionals required to maintain compliance?

F. Public Relations

A joint function of asset management and property manager is to communicate with the larger community. Key questions include:

1. What are the image goals for the property?
2. How to enable a free flow of information between the owner, the asset manager, lenders, public agencies, tenants and neighbors?
3. Is the property perceived to be an asset to the larger community?
4. Is that perception adequately publicized?
5. How does the property enhance the organization's mission and community goals.

G. Disaster Response

In the event of a crisis, whether it involve the physical condition of the property, conditions within the neighborhood, tenant-relations or the finances of the property, Asset Management and Property Management must work together to devise an acceptable and practical solution. Questions include:

1. What are the 3 most likely disasters?
2. What risk control options are available
3. Who should respond, how, and when?
4. What is the evacuation plan?
5. Where are tenants that may require assistance?

*TOP 10 CAPITAL RESERVE ISSUES

Replacement reserves *always* run out—"when?" is the question.

1. No surplus cash flow to fund reserves.

2. No CNA policy guidance from senior management.

3. Required improvements not included in CNA.

4. No one performs capital needs assessments (CNAs).

5. Only half of the components included in reserve calculation.

6. CNAs don't incorporate inflation correctly.

7. CNAs don't consider replacement percentage factors.

8. Reserves expended on maintenance and amenities.

9. No end game plan for refinance or sale.

10. Suicidal underwriting where project expenses exceed income well before 15-, 20-year affordability period.

*Identified by past participants in Asset Management Practicum by URC, Inc.

A SYNDICATOR DISCUSSES PROJECT RESERVES

Reserves are a way of structuring resources for project risk management.

Operating and Lease-Up Reserves—address the risk that project income will be insufficient to fund day to day project requirements.

Replacement Reserves—fund major capital replacement as building components wear out or are damaged.

Other Reserves—for example, for tenant services may also be structured to address specific project needs.

A syndicator would prefer to have very large reserves. These protect the project from economic risks, which help protect the project and the syndicator's return on his investment. A lender prefers debt coverage ratios large enough to protect loans to the project, but usually is not particularly concerned about protecting the limited partner's equity investment. Developers want to minimize reserves. That leaves more in earned fees to use to fund future projects.

Operating Reserves are funded from the investor's equity, but may also come from cash flow. When possible, they are contributed over time so their present value is less, making the overall contribution more efficient and the total equity raised larger.

Historically, the syndicators size the operating reserve two ways:

The operating reserve is keyed to the project's annual operating costs. The size usually is between six months' and one year's operating costs and hard debt service. The precise requirement is a function of project risk and the relative negotiating strength of the parties.

At other times, the project's cash flow is projected for the 15-year initial compliance period, discounted for risk, and the reserve sized to cover the shortfall in adjusted cash flow.

Replacement Reserves may be funded either from cash flow or up-front from investor equity. New construction and vacant-building gut rehab projects typically are funded from cash flow, if cash flow is sufficient. However, partially occupied, mod rehab, and SRO projects may be required to pre-fund all or a portion of their replacement reserves. A partially occupied rehab project may need to draw on replacement reserves earlier than gut rehab or new construction projects, and its replacement needs may occur in a less predictable way. And SRO and other special needs housing may not have cash flow sufficient to fund reserves. Therefore, these kinds of projects often have replacement reserves funded at project closing, in whole or in part.

(SAMPLE) ANNUAL REPLACEMENT RESERVES CASH FLOW DETAILS

Year	1998	1999	2000	2001	2002	2003	2004	2005	2006	2007	2008
STARTING RESERVE BALANCE	$211,485	$218,846	$212,579	$212,579	$202,761	$192,047	$174,934	$154,008	$137,475	$212,021	$84,833
Annual Reserve Contribution	$9,640	$9,640	$9,640	$9,640	$9,640	$9,640	$9,640	$9,640	$9,640	$9,640	$9,640
Interest Earnings	$7,401	$7,660	$7,440	$7,097	$7,097	$6,722	$6,123	$5,390	$4,812	$4,236	$2,969
Reserve Funds Available	$228,506	$236,146	$229,659	$219,493	$219,493	$208,697	$190,697	$169,038	$151,927	$134,897	$97,442

# EXPENDITURES	YEAR 22	YEAR 23	YEAR 24	YEAR 25	YEAR 26	YEAR 27	YEAR 28	YEAR 29	YEAR 30	YEAR 31	YEAR 32
1 Resurface Decks	$0	$0	$0	$0	$0	$5,107	$0	$5,107	$0	$0	$6,066
2 Asphalt	$0	$8,280	$0	$0	$0	$0	$9,834	$0	$0	$0	$0
3 Mail Boxes	$0	$0	$0	$0	$0	$0	$0	$0	$0	$0	$5,642
4 Patio Furniture	$0	$0	$0	$1,885	$0	$0	$0	$0	$2,239	$0	$0
5 Linoleum	$0	$0	$0	$685	$0	$0	$0	$0	$0	$0	$0
6 Intercom System	$0	$0	$0	$0	$0	$0	$0	$0	$0	$0	$2,680
7 Parking Gate Meter	$0	$1,380	$0	$0	$0	$0	$0	$0	$0	$5,452	$0
8 Sprinkler System	$0	$0	$0	$0	$0	$2,375	$0	$0	$0	$0	$0
9 Hot Water Tanks	$0	$0	$0	$0	$0	$0	$0	$0	$0	$0	$0
10 Stucco Repaint	$0	$0	$0	$0	$0	$0	$0	$0	$0	$34,072	$0
11 Parking Space Restripe	$0	$0	$0	$0	$1,148	$0	$0	$0	$0	$0	$1,411
12 Replace Flat Roof	$0	$0	$0	$0	$0	$0	$0	$0	$0	$0	$0
13 Fire Alarm System	$0	$0	$0	$0	$1,148	$0	$0	$0	$0	$0	$1,148
14 Hoses and Extinguishers	$0	$0	$0	$0	$0	$0	$0	$3,817	$0	$0	$0
15 Plumbing Pipes	$0	$0	$14,997	$15,522	$16,065	$16,828	$17,210	$17,812	$18,435	$0	$0
16 Heater Boiler and Pump	$0	$0	$0	$0	$0	$0	$0	$0	$0	$0	$0
17 Carpeting	$0	$0	$8,570	$8,826	$9,090	$9,364	$9,645	$9,934	$10,232	$10,540	$10,856
TOTALS	$0	$9,660	$23,567	$26,898	$27,451	$33,474	$36,689	$31,583	$30,906	$50,064	$27,803
ENDING RESERVE BALANCE	$211,465	$218,846	$212,579	$202,761	$192,047	$174,934	$154,008	$137,475	$121,021	$84,833	$69,839

EXAMPLE
REPLACEMENT RESERVE POLICY

All property managers shall establish within a maximum of 9 months a replacement reserve asset management and maintenance planning program with the following characteristics:

1. *Replacement Calculation Methods.* Each of 60 components in 5 large areas shall be quantified, inspected and aged to identify remaining economic life. This will be done in conjunction with the property maintenance supervisor, the property manager and outside subcontractors maintaining specialized equipment like elevators, boilers, and large air conditioning units at all times.

2. *Inflation.* Our policy is to use the 50-year rate of inflation in the housing and construction industry. Our current calculation is 2.9% per Means Cost Data. We will be using 3% for the inflation rate for all future costs.

3. *Renovation Style.* The renovation shall be performed with multiple styles. Appliance and individual apartment equipment shall be replaced on a 7-year normal curve. Up to the point at which 50% of the items are scheduled for failure, wholesale replacement will be assumed.

4. *Refinance Period.* The refinancing and transfer of the property to the real estate preservation or redevelopment department shall begin approximately 3 years prior to the loss crossover point. In any case, when the unfunded actual requirements and potential improvements exceed $700,000 or $22,000 per unit, the properties must be scheduled for refinance.

5. *Economic Life Evaluation.* We shall use the midpoint of a 5 point visual assessment scale to estimate the remaining economic life.

6. *Future Improvements.* In all cases, at least a 10% above the known improvement costs shall be included as a contingency, not only for construction requirements, but for additional code items. This is to be used as a minimum where older properties might require

being renovated up to conformance with: current law; life safety; accessibility; antidiscrimination, or energy standards. Significant additional items may be required of up to 30% more than the current reserve calculation costs.

7. *CNA Review Period.* Each year, the property supervisor, property manager and asset manager shall meet and create a spreadsheet or database listing proactive maintenance items and potential eligibility for funding from the replacement reserve in light of the next 15 year outlays.

8. *Policy Review Period.* These policies shall remain in effect for the next 5 years whereupon they must be reviewed, endorsed, modified and edited by the senior management, board of directors and tenant organization.

Attachment 2-1:
HOME Provisions Needed in a Written Agreement
between Owner and Property Manager

When the property management of a HOME-assisted property is contracted out, HUD expects the owner and property manager to enter into an agreement or contract to ensure that the property is operated satisfactorily and in compliance with the HOME Program requirements. The written agreement or contract is a legal document that the owner can use to convey the HOME requirements and the owner's performance expectations to the property manager. This checklist can be used by owners to ensure that their written agreements with property managers include all the terms and provisions that are necessary to manage HOME-assisted properties in compliance with HOME requirements.

Is this item included in the written agreement?	Yes / No
Roles and responsibilities of each party	
Owner's performance goals and performance standards and the manager's corresponding responsibilities	
Requirement to adhere to the management plan *Note: The management plan should include detailed guidance on how to manage the property, including how to comply with the HOME requirements. A key term of the written agreement should be compliance with the management plan.*	
HOME affordability requirements:	
• Duration of affordability period	
• Number of High HOME Rent units and Low HOME Rent units that must be maintained through the affordability period and property-specific guidance that describes how to maintain the unit mix	
• Guidance on how to use the HOME income limits:	
– Income targeting (how many households at what income levels must occupy the High HOME Rent units and Low HOME Rent units)	
– Determining initial income-eligibility, including definition of household income and acceptable source documents	
– Certifying continued income-eligibility, including acceptable method of income recertification	
• Establishing rents	
– Using HOME rent limits	
– Using the utility allowance, if applicable	
– Initial rents that can be charged	
– Rent increases, including when rents can be increased and procedures for securing owner and/or PJ approval of rent increases	
Tenant selection terms, including occupancy rules of HOME, the application process, tenant selection procedures	
Lease terms, including the length of the lease, prohibited lease clauses, and who approves the lease	

**Attachment 2-1: HOME Provisions Needed in a Written Agreement
between Owner and Property Manager** *(continued)*

Is this item included in the written agreement?	Yes / No
Lease enforcement, including property manager's responsibility for monitoring tenant compliance with leases, what constitutes "good cause" for tenant evictions, and process for evictions	
Nondiscrimination provisions	
Marketing, including affirmative marketing requirements (for properties with five or more units) and marketing accessible units, if applicable	
Maintaining the property and making repairs	
• Meeting applicable property standards, including lead-based paint requirements	
• Identification of who performs maintenance tasks, who has authority to approve repairs, make capital expenditures, etc.	
• Service request response times	
• Providing utilities and services	
Managing property finances to ensure continued financial viability and operation as affordable housing	
• Operating budget and operating account disbursements (guidance on using property operating funds)	
• Rent collections and other accounts receivables	
• Accounting and bookkeeping requirements	
• Insurance	
Reporting to the owner and/or to the PJ, including what financial, maintenance, and rent and occupancy reports are required; who must prepare them; and to whom must they be submitted	
Record-keeping, including a description of tenant, property, and marketing files that must be maintained; for how long; and who has access	
Guidelines for staffing, to ensure adequate maintenance and compliance with HOME requirements:	
• The type and number of employees working at the property	
• Whether staff, such as an on-site manager or maintenance worker, will reside at the property, and if so, on what terms. (Note, due to a conflict of interest, the owner(s) and other employees, agents, and consultants should not reside at the property.)	
• Employee compensation	
• Payment of applicable payroll taxes, workers compensation insurance, health insurance, and other employee benefits	
Legal enforcement provisions (how the owner will enforce the agreement if the property manager does not comply with its terms or meet performance standards)	
Conditions under which the agreement will be terminated	
Additional requirements imposed by the PJ and/or the owner on the project	

Attachment 2-2:
Sample Monthly/Quarterly Report
from the Property Manager to the Owner

Property Name:
Property Manager:
Reporting Period:

Indicator	Month 1	Month 2	Month 3
Gross Potential Rent			
Percentage of Gross Potential Rent Collected			
Total Income			
Total Expenditures			
Cash Balance (end of month)			
Accounts Receivable (end of month)			
Accounts Payable (end of month)			
Capital Reserve Account Total			
Vacancies (end of month)			

List all units that are off-line with an explanation and length of time off-line.

List findings from the last physical inspection and current status, as of the end of the quarter.

Attachment 2-3:
Records that the Property Manager Must Retain

	Key HOME Requirement	Documentation
Initial Applicant Eligibility	• 100% of households at or below 80% area median income (AMI) • Initially, 90% of households at or below 60% AMI • If 5 or more HOME-assisted units, Low HOME Rent units occupied by households at or below 50% AMI • Income determined using PJ-provided/HOME allowable definition, verified by source documents at tenants' initial occupancy	• Completed application in the project file • Source documentation (wage statements, interest statements) in the project file • Completed calculation of household income • Determination of eligibility (based on current HOME income limits)
Continued Tenant Income Eligibility	• 100% of households at or below 80% area median income (AMI) • If 5 or more HOME-assisted units, Low HOME Rent units occupied by households at or below 50% AMI • Income determined using PJ-provided/HOME allowable definition, verified by method adopted by the PJ	• Tenant files documenting annual income certification • Every 6th year, source documentation (wage statements, interest statements) in the project file • Completed calculation of household income • Determination of eligibility (based on current HOME income limits)
Rents	• Low HOME Rents: 30% of tenant income, or 30% of income of a household at or below 50% AMI, or the rent allowable under project-based subsidy program, as determined by the PJ • If 5 or more HOME-assisted units, 20% of units must be at or below Low HOME Rents • High HOME Rents: based on lesser of FMR or 30% of income at 65% AMI	• Rent and occupancy reports, documenting High and Low HOME Rent units • Documentation of current, applicable High and Low HOME Rent limits used to determine rents • Documentation of utility allowances used to determine rents • Completed calculation of rent determination • Tenant leases documenting actual rents charged • Annual Rent Roll
Maintaining Unit Mix	• Take appropriate steps for maintaining unit mix, as needed for fixed or floating HOME units • Increase rent for tenants whose incomes exceed 80% AMI	• Rent and occupancy reports to show unit designations and redesignations • Tenant files and leases documenting rent increases
Fair Housing and Affirmative Marketing	• If 5 or more HOME-assisted units, follow PJ affirmative marketing procedures • Nondiscrimination in all rental activities	• Documentation showing all advertising and outreach activities
Tenant Protections	• Leases for at least one year; PJ approval required for shorter lease • Fair and equitable tenant selection policy • Written notification to rejected applicants	• Tenant selection policy • All prospective tenant applications and correspondence • Tenant files, including tenant leases • Documentation of PJ approval for any leases less than one year

Property Standards	• Continued compliance with applicable codes and standards:
	  – Acquisition: state/local codes
	  – Rehabilitation: state/local codes or national model code, rehab standards
	  – New construction: state/local codes or national model code, rehab standards, International Energy Conservation Code, UFAS (for accessible units)
		• Document state/local code, model code, and/or written rehabilitation standard provided by PJ
		• Documentation of work on property, work orders, capital improvements

Chapter 2

ASSET MANAGEMENT HANDBOOK

AN ASSET MANAGEMENT PLAN & PORTFOLIO WORKBOOK

Theme:	They call it a workbook because you must work to gain the ultimate benefit.
Learning Objectives:	• To Introduce Layout and Format of Workbook and Narrative Report
	• To Define Asset Management Plan Components
	• To Identify Benchmarking Opportunities
Essential Vocabulary:	— Persistence
	— Certificate of Occupancy
	— Asset Management Plan
	— Benchmarking Plan
	— Monitoring Plan
	— PUPA
	— Preventative Maintenance
	— Disaster Response

RENTAL PROPERTY LIFE CYCLE

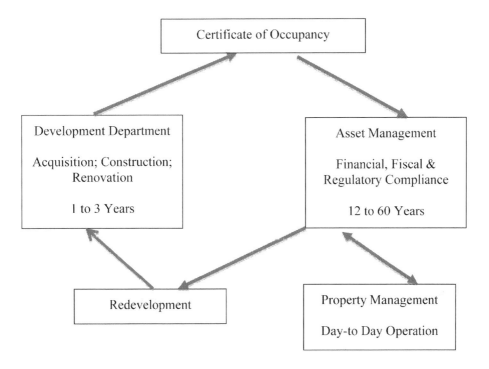

RENTAL PROPERTY LIFE CYCLE

The day a property receives its Certificate of Occupancy is the day it begins to depreciate. For hopefully longer than 12 years and up to 40 years, the property stays healthy and well ahead of rising expenses and depreciating components. Two primary actors form a team: the property manager works day to day and thinks "long-term" is a year and the asset manager looks far ahead, at least 5 to 15 years into the future. When they agree that the property must be refinanced and redeveloped, they hand it off to the development or preservation department. This department applies for financing, takes control of the property and completes the reconstruction. At the end of the reconstruction period, the property has a new life and the cycle begins again.

In the nonprofit world, this is an infinite loop because there is no objective to sell the properties to produce income.

A PORTFOLIO MANAGEMENT PLAN

A LIST OF RECOMMENDED COMPONENTS

Overall Asset

1. Initial Development Proforma

2. 20-Year Operating Budget Projection

3. Capital Finance Plan

4. Refinance Plan

5. Monitoring Plan

6. Benchmarking Plan with Risk Ranking

The Physical Elements

1. Capital Needs Projections

2. Preventative Maintenance Plan

3. Disaster Response Plan

AN ASSET MANAGEMENT PLAN

THE FINANCING PLAN
Edited from CHAM

An Asset Management Plan includes at least 6 components.

1. **The Development Proforma**. This is the Financial Sources and Uses spreadsheet recording for how the property will be acquired and built. It includes realistic estimates for all costs: construction, property acquisition, and soft costs that go into a development effort. With respect to the construction costs, a very important issue is the quality and ease of maintenance of the materials and equipment Paying for high quality, low maintenance, long lasting materials and equipment is costly on the front end. But it saves significant annual costs and typically enhances the values of the asset over the long run. In addition, residents surrounded by first class equipment tend to take good care of it, which helps the manager keep the development in excellent condition.

2. **The Twenty Year Operating Budget Projection**. It is vital to make the most educated guesses about what costs will look like over the affordability period. At the base level, this means estimating the rate at which rents and operating costs will rise. On the income side, the real question is any subsidy program involved in the development. Many of these have time limits of anywhere from five and twenty years (e.g. the length of Section 8 or McKinny Section 8 contracts). As much as owners may be confident of renewals, the long range financial plan must be conservative and assume that source of subsidy may end after the contract period.

What Types of Information Should the Owner Track to Ensure Property Financial Viability?

The owner should routinely review the property manager's adherence to the budgets that have been established, and the property's cash flow. Operational issues to consider in undertaking a cash flow analysis are:

Gross potential rent income
   for HOME-assisted and
   non-assisted units;
Non-housing services costs;
Security costs;
Rent loss;
Normal repair costs;
Vacancy loss;
Real estate taxes;
Utility costs;
Concession loss;
Property insurance;

Bad debt loss;
Liability insurance;
Other income;
Capital expenditures;
Marketing expenses;
Net operating income;
Payroll expenses;
Debt service; and
Property management fee;
Asset management costs.
Other administrative expense

3. **A Capital Finance Plan**. All real estate ages, depreciates, and requires rebuilding. Good quality construction and excellent maintenance can make that aging process gentle and tolerable for residents. But the time will come when major repairs must be made.

   The primary solution is the capital reserve fund. The extended operating budget projections must show that the fund will have grown to a level that will allow for the future cost of the repair or replacement.

   A capital financing plan can also be based on collateral other than the property. This might mean the selling or mortgaging of some other property,—a separate fund-raising effort. If this is the plan, a similar set of questions needs to be asked and answered. A Capital Finance Plan must be updated every 3 years. What is important is to have a plan. Then, as things change, the owner and the manager will have an idea of how they must adjust to the new situations.

4. **A Refinancing Plan**. It is unusual for a subsided real estate to be built, have the loan paid off, and operate debt-free for any substantial period of time. Another solution is to plan for refinancing the property. Will there be enough equity in the property at the time the capital improvement is anticipated? Can the property bear the added payments for the new loan? Does the currently planned permanent financing allow such new borrowing? There are a number of questions such as these to be answered if refinancing is the plan.

5. **The Monitoring Plan.** Every owner must ensure that its assisted property complies with all funding requirements.

Owners often hire professional property managers (as staff or contractors) to operate their rental properties for them. Even with property management staff or contractors, the *owner* is accountable for compliance with the federal requirements. Owners must understand the requirements, manage the property per the requirements, compile accurate and timely reports, and maintain records and documentation of their compliance efforts. The tools available to the owner to hold the property manager accountable for compliance are: written agreements, reporting, and monitoring.

What Should the Owner Monitor?

At a minimum, the Asset Manager should review the performance of the property manager in the following key areas:

Adherence to income limits, rent limits, and occupancy standards;
Financial management, including rent collections and cash controls;
Physical management, including routine maintenance, capital planning, and property standards;
Adherence to lease and tenant rights requirements; and
Affirmative marketing.

6. **The Benchmarking Plan.** The analysis of the industry provides benchmarks against which a business can be measured. Benchmarks can be financial (balance sheet, profit and loss account) and operational ratios such as staffing ratios, vacancy rate and other relevant measures. Some industries are driven by key ratios: for example, apartment owners measure occupancy rates, airlines measure load factors and TV channels measure viewer ratings.

Benchmarking is useful both for business operations and to develop objectives:

- Typically bankers and other financial shareholders will evaluate your proforma against known numbers from your competitors. If key ratios in your proforma are substantially different from the industry norm, you must provide a good reason for this.

- Industry benchmarks provide ranges for your business.

- Benchmarks identify a best practice and provide targets for improvement. For example, if a competitor achieves a higher occupancy rate, this higher number can become an objective in your strategic plan. You know that it is achievable because a competitor has achieved it.

IREM and CHAM have formed a "benchmarking database". Competitors would supply agreed operational statistics at certain intervals to the trusted third party. The trusted third party would compute values for the "best in class", the average and the worst, without identifying the company to which the data relates. This amalgamated data is sold back to all club members so that they can make comparison on how well they are doing. The advantage is that the benchmarks are well defined and usually not available from any other source.

PROPERTY BENCHMARKING GOALS

Address _____ **Date** _____

	BEST PRACTICE	NOTES
OPERATIONS		
1a. Expenses to Income	Income exceeds all cash expenses including reserves	
1b. Total Operating Cost PUPA	75% of area, less than 85% of income	
2. Accounts Payable	100% within 60 days 85% within 30 days	
3. Occupancy Rate	95%	
4. Rent Collection	95% Tenant 100% Subsidy	
5. Eviction Timing	Within 5 days of legal date	
6. Turnaround Time	80%—3-15 business days 20%—10-15 business days	
7. Work Order Systems		
- Emergency Response	24 hours	
- Vacancy Refurbishment	3-15 business days	
- Preventative	90% within 2 weeks of schedule	
- Planned	Within 5 days of schedule	
- Tenant Requests	Within 3-7 business days	
8. Energy Conservation	Annual consumption/cost analysis	
9. Management Plan	Updated annually	
10. Tenant Satisfaction	90% annual tenant satisfaction surveys	
11. Turnover Rate	Less than 20%	
12. Operating Reserves	10-25% per your of annual operating budget	
13. Reporting to Investors/ Lenders/Regulators	Within 5 days of reporting deadlines	
*14.		

	BEST PRACTICE	NOTES
ASSET PRESERVATION		
1. Replacement Reserves	Sufficient reserves to cover next major expense per CNA	
	CNA updated every 5 years	
	RR balance per CNA	
	RR Annual $	
2. *Maintenance*		
- Unit Inspections	Annual unit inspections	
- Preventative Maintenance	Preventative maintenance plan	
- % Tenant Maintenance	Less than 20% of total	
- Maintenance Budget PUPA	Between $3,800 & $7,000	
3. Disposition and Refinancing Plan	Disposition and/or refinancing plan in place	
*4.		
RESIDENT RELATIONS & SERVICES		
Newsletter/Blog	Monthly distribution	
# of police calls per month	Under 1 per 100 units/week	
Meeting Participation	20% or 90% of invited	
Employment %	Increasing	
Savings Club	96% achievement of goal	
Day Care	80% of max capacity	
Transportation	2 times/week	
*8.		
*9.		
MANAGEMENT		
1. Proforma vs. Current Rent	1.0 or higher	
2. Insurance Assessment	Annual review	
3. Disaster Planning	Fire drill, disaster plan, annual review	
4. Budget	+/-4% annual	
*5.		

*Blank fields are for your property-specific benchmarking goals

EXAMPLE
DETAILED RISK RANKING REPORT

RISK	ADDRESS: 1703-B Front Street				CURRENT STATUS
	2009	2010	2011	2012	
Vacancy	5	4	4	5	18% vacancy
Collection Loss	5	4	4	5	21% loss
Cash Flow	4	3	4	5	Negative $6,000
Reserves	4	4	5	5	Not funded
Debt Coverage Ratio	5	5	5	5	Below 1.0
Sponsor Capacity	3	2	2	2	Showing strain
Asset Management	3	3	2	2	Just starting
Property Management	2	2	2	2	No major
Reporting	3	3	3	2	Late but accurate
Physical Condition	3	3	3	4	Showing age
Benchmarks	3	3	4	5	50%

Outstanding (1); Strong (2); Performing (3); Marginal (4); Salvageable (5); Probable Loss (6)

THE PHYSICAL ELEMENTS

1). CAPITAL NEEDS PROJECTIONS

The construction of a capital improvement plan requires a team that understands physical development. It begins with creating a spreadsheet of all the components of the property, and determining their natural life expectancy. The roof system is likely to have a life expectancy of 20 years and its replacement will be costly. The structural system is likely to have a life expectancy of 75 years or more. Planning for its replacement requires a team that understands physical development and financial projections. Thinking about capital improvements is most easily done by systems. Various parts of the system have different life expectancies (e.g. the boiler may wear out before the piping). Concrete plans need to be made for each component. Following is a list of the major areas that should be addressed:

1. Envelope: Siding, Roofing, Windows, Doors

2. Site: Parking, Play Area, Drives, Lighting

3. Common Areas: Office, Hall, Laundry

4. Mechanical/Electrical: Plumbing, Electrical, HVAC, Elevators

5. Unit Interiors: Kitchen, Bath, Floors, Doors, Walls

6. Forecast Improvements: Code, Accessibility, Sustainability, Energy, Technology

CURRENT CONDITION?

Components quantities are identified and entered into a prepared spreadsheet template. The next step is to determine the remaining life expectancies under current condition. Preventive maintenance plan should be put in place to assure that the components can, in fact, serve the property and its residents cost effectively for the full length of their anticipated life.

FINANCING SOURCES

Finally, 40 year capital improvement plan should be scheduled, cost estimated and fed into the financial plan and refinancing plan.

2). PREVENTIVE MAINTENANCE PLAN

The preventive maintenance plan is the core of the comprehensive maintenance plan. The preventive maintenance effort helps assure the building components remain efficient throughout their projected useful life. Preventive maintenance usually provides a very significant return on investment.

AN ANNUAL PLAN

Components that require a preventive maintenance schedule:

1. Elevators
2. Weather protection (siding, roofing, windows, doors, flashing)
3. Security (alarms, locks, cameras)
4. Auxiliary, backup, and emergency systems
5. Heating, ventilating and air conditioning (boiler, piping, valves, pumps, radiators or equivalent, filters, fans, compressors)
6. Fire equipment (extinguishers, alarms, hoses, pumps)
7. Solid waste disposal systems (compactors, dumpsters, chutes)
8. Power (wiring, transformers, generators)
9. Water and sewers (piping, pumps, valves)
10. Interior surfaces (carpet, tile, wood)
11. Vehicles (cars, trucks, mowers, sweepers, plows)
12. Plant material (trees, shrubs, flowers, grass)
13. Site furniture (lighting, seating, play equipment)

MONTHLY ENFORCEMENT

Manufacturers' manuals describe the required actions and the time interval between them. Effective owners and their property and asset management team develop a preventive maintenance calendar before the property opens. And then the instructions to the staff are clear indications this task is second in importance only to emergencies and vacancy preparation. Most preventive maintenance tasks are simple. Involves lubricating, changing a filter, or inspecting and cleaning. There is no "squeaky wheel." Preventive maintenance schedule of the activities without supervision and consistent enforcement are useless.

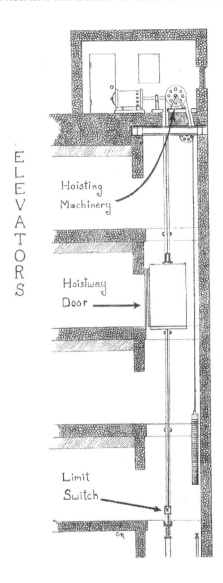

E
L
E
V
A
T
O
R
S

Hoisting
Machinery

Hoistway
Door →

Limit
Switch

MAINTENANCE MATTERS

Elevators are an example of equipment that responds notoriously well to preventative maintenance. Maintenance contracts can be very expensive due to the critical nature of the service and requirements for licensed individuals. It is not an area to economize as the entire building can become untenable if this one piece of equipment fails. In figuring future replacements, if you only have 1 elevator, I always recommend adding a second when refinancing the property.

3). DISASTER RESPONSE PLAN

ProActive

Disasters may involve the physical condition of the property, neighborhood situations, tenant-relations or finances. Asset Management and Property Management must work together to devise an acceptable and practical solution. The plan must clearly identify the following:

1. Of the 10 most damaging potential situations, which 3 are most likely disasters?
2. What are the lines of emergency communication and authority
3. What risk control options are available
4. Who should respond, how, and when?
5. When is the evaluation plan to be instituted?
6. Where are tenants that may require physical assistance?
7. How often should the plan be reviewed and approved by the board and tenant representatives?

ASSET MANAGEMENT WORKBOOK
TEMPORARY TABLE OF CONTENTS

This document is available for download at the website for this book

I.   Format

- Your Cover Page
- Contents
- Portfolio Executive Summary

II.   Portfolio Overview

A. CNA Policies & Assumption Worksheet

B. Portfolio Risk Ranking Narrative
   Portfolio Status—Ranking Table
   Rankings (definitions)

C. Portfolio Performance Narrative
   Portfolio Benchmarking Summary

D. Portfolio Capital Plan
- Recapitalization Year & Amount

E. Portfolio Action Plan

III.   Case Study / Initial Property

- Table of Contents

A. Property Synopsis
B. Executive Summary
C. Property Background/Status
D. Property Objectives
E. Property Risk & Performance Rating Narrative
- Detailed Risk Ranking Template
- Property Performance Analysis Template

F. CNA Narrative Discussion
G. Operating Status Narrative
H. Project Recapitalization Sources
I. Property Action Plan
• Work Plan

ASSET MANAGEMENT REPORT EXAMPLE

- **SYNOPSIS AND PROPERTY PERFORMANCE**
- **NARRATIVE**
- **ACTION PLAN**

The following example is derived from a real property. It has a positive view of 3 aspects of an asset management report. The first is a concise synopsis including performance standards. The second is a narrative of the objective analysis of the current conditions of the property; both a risk ranking and benchmarking overview, along with the goals, assumptions, and policies this organization used followed by reserve and recapitalization plans. The last section represents an action plan from the asset manager to be jointly carried out by the ownership and property management division.

ANNUAL ASSET MANAGEMENT REPORT

Uptown Homes Limited Partnership Company
Action Housing Corporation Lease Purchase Development

CONTENTS

I. **Overview**

> Property Synopsis
> Performance Standards

II. **Narrative**

> A.   Project Background
> B.   Asset Management Objectives
> C.   Current Condition
> D.   Property CNA Policies
> E.   Reserve Status
> F.   Exist Strategy/Recapitalization Plan

III. **Action Plans**

> Annual Action Plan

Completed by: *Eric Fromm*

Date: *April 3, 2004*

ASSET MANAGEMENT
I. PROPERTY SYNOPSIS

UPTOWN HOMES LPC

Address: Scattered Site—See Schedule					
Tax Parcel Id#: Varies					
Exempt (partial or full) and if so, tax registration #: Partial—50%					
Legal Description: Varies					
Onsite Manager (yes or no): Dedicated but off site					
Date Constructed: 2001					
Date Acquired: 2001					
Unit Type	**# of Units**	**# of Bedrooms / Baths**	**% of AIM**	**Rent**	**Utilities included in rent?**
SFD	20	4/3	40%	$785	$0
SFD	20	3/12	40%	$610	$0
SFD	9	5/3	40%	$900	$0
Total	49				
Note: Lease purchase in East Creek					
Resident Profile	Large families; 50% Hispanic; 10% disabled				
Description	Low income homeownership opportunity				
Financial Structure	Syndicated with leasing cooperative				
1ˢᵗ Mortgage	Wells Fargo Investments—$2,935,000 due 2015, payable PITI @ 7.3% monthly				
2ⁿᵈ Mortgage	City of Beaufort—$1,230,000 deferred payment. HOME funds restricted affordability until 2021				
3ʳᵈ Mortgage	Partner Exit Taxes—unknown due 2016 if purchase option is enacted				
Major Issues	Replacement shortfall (roofing @ $216,000) in 2012 and exit tax payment ($600,000?)				
Assessed Value	$4.16 million				
Benchmarks	Good—6/2004 @ 90%; $2,000 cash flow; reserves unfunded				
Updated/By	R.M. Santucci—April 2004				

PROPERTY PERFORMANCE STANDARDS

Uptown Homes Limited Partnership Company   **Date:** 06/04

	INDUSTRY STANDARD	2003-2004 PERFORMANCE	X
OPERATIONS			
1a. Expenses to Income	Income exceeds all expenses including reserves	X $2,000	
1b. Total Operating Cost PUPA	75% of area	$3,845	
2. Accounts Payable	Bills paid 100% within 60 days	X	
	85% within 30 days	X	
3. Occupancy Rate	95%	98%	
4. Rent Collection	95% Tenant	99%	
	100% Subsidy	100%	
5. Eviction Timing	Within 5 days of legal date _____	None	
6. Turnaround Time	90%—3-10 business days	80%—10 days	
	10%—10-15 business days	X	
7. Work Order Systems			
- Emergency	24 hours	X	
- Vacancy Refurbishment	3-15 business days	X	
- Preventative	Within 2 weeks of schedule	X	
- Planned	Within 5 days of schedule	X	
- Tenant Requests	3-7 business days	X	
8. Energy Conservation	Annual consumption/cost analysis	X	
9. Management Plan	Updated annually	X	
10. Tenant Satisfaction	Annual tenant satisfaction surveys	Every other year	
11. Turnover Rate	Less than 20%	12%	
12. Operating Reserves	10-25% per your of annual operating budget	6%	
13. Reporting to Investors/ Lenders/Regulators	Within 5 days of reporting deadlines	X	

	INDUSTRY STANDARD	2003—2004 PERFORMANCE	X
ASSET PRESERVATION			
1. Replacement Reserves	- Sufficient reserves to cover next major problem	No/short $260,000 Roof replacement	
	- CNA updated every 5 years	X	
	- RR balance per CNA	X	
	- RR being funded	X	
2. *Maintenance* Unit Inspections Preventative Maintenance % Tenant Maintenance Total Maintenance Budget PUPA	Annual unit inspections	X	
	Preventative maintenance plan	X	
	Less than 20% of total	24%	
	Between $3,800 & $7,000	$2,000	
3. Disposition and Refinancing	Disposition and/or plan in place	In process	

II. EXAMPLE NARRATIVE

A. *Project Background*

The Action Housing Corporation (AHC) is the nonprofit sponsor for Uptown Homes Limited Partnership (UHLP) project. UHLP consists of 49 scattered site single—family homes, with three and four bedrooms, located throughout the Beaufort target area constructed in 2001. AHC established a wholly owned subsidiary, Uptown Homes that owns 1% of the UHLP. Therefore, for purposes of this plan, UHLP is viewed as the "owner" of the project. The residents have all executed lease-purchase agreements and are members of the Homeowner's Association.

B. *Asset Management Objectives*

1) Lease units to people with income levels less than 60% of Carteret County area median income and rent levels affordable to people earning 41% of less of the area median income.

2) Physically maintain the assets in the partnership.

3) Maintain lease obligations.

4) Maintain Section 42 and HOME compliance requirements.

5) Maintain fiscal control over operations and partnership disposition strategy, to include identifying financial obligations of holding property to end of partnership and what it means financially to AHC.

6) Organize resident councils.

7) Sell the properties to the residents in Year 16 of the partnership.

8) Create organizational philosophy regarding the Lease Purchase Model of affordable housing on Board level.

9) Create exit strategy that reflects our empowerment philosophy upon termination of the partnership in 2014.

C. *2004 Condition*

1. Risk Rating "Performing". The primary areas to monitor in the future include the debt coverage ratio. It will be difficult to continue to maintain a 1.1 in the face of cost increases on the operating side, specifically insurance and common area utilities, both of which have been inflating in the 10%—20% per year while the proforma rent increase is 2%.

2. Performance Standard Benchmarking. The property is performing extremely well versus the established benchmarks. We have a positive cash flow of approximately $2,000 last year with a very high occupancy and rent collection. The turnaround time is excellent as is the work order system.

   The areas we are working to improve are the operating reserves that have dropped to 6% of the annual budget, and the capital replacement reserves.

3. Capital Needs. Based on recent calculations of the 15-year capital needs assessment, the replacement reserve has a shortfall of approximately $260,000. The next major replacement item will be the roofs in 2012. At $290,000, only $24,000 is available. Because these units are being prepared for sale to the tenants, there is a relatively low maintenance budget and the occupants perform a great deal of the traditional preventative maintenance.

4. 4) Disposition Plan. One of the major items to develop in the future is a full disposition plan identifying the various prices, benefits and costs to both UHLP and the occupant cooperator. Attachment A contains a summary of 14 performance standards that are being measured for this project.

D. *Property CNA Policies*

We use life cycle costs to calculate our replacement reserve.

Our rate of inflation is 2.9% or 3%.

We replace our stove and refrigerators over a 3-year curve. All other items in single years.

What is our required precision in evaluating economic life? Field map

When replacement needs are projected to exceed $750,000, we will refinance.

We grade and analyze the remaining economic life of our building using a 5 point visual inspection and the FNMA life span table.

How shall we incorporate, know and project additional standards into our CNA? Add all current code requirements; allow 6% for a market updates, create 10% universal design units.

What is capital and what is maintenance? All replacement turnovers are maintenance until Year 10. Exterior and common areas painting are capital at Years 6, 12, 18.

E. *Reserve Status*

Operating Reserves: The loan agreement requires initial funding of $58,000; thereafter, 1% of Effective Gross Rent Collections shall be contributed to this fund as long as there is sufficient cash flow available. As of December 31, 2004, the operating reserve is under funded by $4,600.

Replacement Reserves: The loan agreement requires initial funding of $49,000; thereafter, $250 per unit per year, or flat amount of $12,250 each year of Net Operating Income Less allocation for real estate taxes and insurance escrow. This reserve is under funded by $25,000, $12,250 for 2000 and 2001. It was reported that the reserves were fully funded in Spring of 2002 by deferred equity.

UHLP is currently investigating ways to fund the replacement of the roofs in 2012 through additional replacement deposits, preventative maintenance and outside capital grants.

Both reserves have to be funded prior to any payment of deferred development and partnership management fees. (See 30-Year Capital Needs Assessment: Summary and Project Replacement Reserve Details)

F. *Exit Strategy/Recapitalization Plan*

In Year 15 (2014), the units in UHLP will be sold to AHC for outstanding debt plus partnership exit taxes. The lease purchase option prices will be established in part using these costs. Since AHC's Subsidiary, UHLP, is responsible for paying exit taxes, it's in AHC's best interest to minimize them. This is accomplished by maintaining the LP Capital account at or above a "zero" balance. The syndicator has underwritten this project with the expectation that the LP account will become negative in 2014. This should he monitored by UHLP's auditor and Syndicator. A projection of exit taxes in Year 15 should be prepared and reviewed on an annual basis for disposition planning purposes.

III. UPTOWN HOMES ACTION PLAN

— Refinance the existing first mortgage now with rates at an all time low. Savings will result in additional net operating income.

— The Limited Partner Capital account needs to remain positive and will need to be monitored annually to ensure exit taxes are minimized.

— Develop a financing plan for lease purchasers in Uptown Homes LP for the Year 16 holding period that reflects sales per year and holding costs. Identify local banks that can be involved in creating tools for this plan.

— Creating an education plan leading up to Year 16 so that lease purchasers are capable homeowners by August 7th.

— A timeframe for implementing the Lease Option Agreement needs to be drafted and adopted by June 15th.

— A community awareness plan involving the county, real estate professionals and appraisers should be considered for Year 16 around the impact on local market values when this volume of homes transfers ownership.

Chapter 3

ASSET MANAGEMENT HANDBOOK

BENCHMARKING YOUR PROPERTY

Theme: How are we doing compared to best practices?

Learning Objectives:

- Understand Operating and Asset Preservation Benchmarks

- Consider using Service Program Benchmarks

- Develop Local Benchmark

- Identify Specific Areas of Excellence and

Improvement

Essential Vocabulary:

— Benchmark
— Performance Standard
— Mean
— Mode
— 70 Percentile
— Turnover Cost
— Tenant Receivables
— Accounts Payable
— Resident Services

BENCHMARKS

Benchmarking stems from a historical process where a worker would throw a piece of lumber or a finished product against a mark or stop in their workbench to verify that it is within tolerance. You wouldn't necessarily throw away the expensive piece, especially if it was completed. You would use the information to adjust your crafting process so that the end products were very similar. This is what you are doing when you benchmark your property against known best practices.

BENCHMARKS FOR COMPREHENSIVE PROPERTY MANAGEMENT

Modified from *"A Guide to Comprehensive Asset and Property Management"*

Overview

- Benchmarks provide objective measures against which the asset manager can assess management effectiveness.

- Performance standards may be required by the lender, subsidy source, or equity partner.

- Each property should develop site specific benchmarks.

- A benchmark is not an absolute measure of success or failure. It provides an objective starting point for discussion and analysis of performance.

Analysis and Response

Any benchmark in a field as complex and subjective as property management should act as starting points for discussion and analysis rather than conclusive evidence of success or failure. If, for example, the benchmark for occupancy is 95% and the results for a particular development at the end of the fiscal year are 87%, this is not grounds for immediate removal of the management team. Rather, it suggests further analysis.

Example Analysis

— Was the problem the number of vacancies, or the average length of each vacancy?

— Was the waiting list adequate throughout the year?

— Were there a high number of refusals once offers were made?

— Was there a particular size or location of unit that created a large part of the problem?

— Was there new competition in the neighborhood say of affordable units that were better located, larger, more attractive, less expensive or equipped with more amenities?

— Were there events in this property or its neighborhood that make people reluctant to live here?

— Does management have an efficient system for identifying, refurbishing and reoccupying vacancies?

— Is there a plan in place to achieve or revise the standard?

The analysis of these and similar questions helps the asset manager and the management company develop a strategy for meeting achievable standard in the coming year. Each benchmark has a similar set of analytical questions that are asked in order to probe any gaps between the originally established goal and the actual achievement. Standards are frequently different for various properties in the owner's or manager's portfolio.

Resident Services

The traditional standard for service programs has been the number of people served. A new approach asks what are the *results*. Objective results are the product of many factors and not just the programs at the housing development. Many property managers and owners are resistant to these measures and actively debate their roles in enhancing tenants lives. The following benchmarks are potential areas for measurement:

— Level of participation in resident activities

— Level of participation in neighborhood activities

— Youth graduating from high school

— Adults in the work force

— Number of criminal incidents

— Number of vandalism incidents

— Number of teenage births

— Percentage of children receiving all inoculations

— Participation in sustainability program

— Participation in recycling program

  Total energy use by units

— Participation in annual or quarterly resident meetings

— Student achievement of satisfactory grade levels

— Participation in athletic events and training

RAPID OPERATING ANALYSIS

Using your annual and last month's operating statement for your case study and at least one other property. Fill in the following information:

Property: _____

Total PUPA Costs without Mortgage $_____

Utility Cost PUPA $_____

Management Fee   %_____ $_____ per unit

Insurance Cost $_____ per annum

Property Tax PUPA $_____

Largest other Expense Item $_____for_____

\# Turnovers in last 12 months   _____

Average fix-up cost $_____ PU

Rent loss per average turnover $_____

Call 2 buildings in your service area for market comp rents:

$_____for_____bedrooms
with/ without_____

$_____for_____bedrooms
with/ without_____

*PUPA=per unit per annum

INITIAL ANALYSIS TO IDENTIFY ISSUES

Identify Leaks First!

Identify areas where the properties are losing money. Where either income has fallen or expenses have risen.

Benchmark with Performance Standards.

Compare operating and capital outlays against the 27 standards.

Rent & Amenity Comparison?

A comparison of your unit rent to market rate units to identify how many dollars you are below or above market. How do your amenities hold up compared to new units?

Local Absorption Rate?

Quantify whether the local rental market is hot, medium or cold. What is the absorption rate for your kind of units?

Current versus Initial Performa?

Compare your current operating budget to the first year actual operating budget. It is oft times very illuminating to identify the major line item differences from the new project to one that is now 12, 15 or 20 years old. Some of what you will identify are bad assumptions. Other times, it is inflation in the cost of items over time.

Energy Use

Compare water, sewer, power, and gas costs. What is inflation and what is additional usage? Request an audit or usage review.

OPERATING ISSUES FROM PAST PARTICIPANTS IN URC'S PORTFOLIO ASSET MANAGEMENT PRACTICUM

– Rising utility costs—water, electric, gas, oil
– Insurance major cost increases
– Section 8 vouchers are shrinking in number
– Tenant receivables increasing to 20%
– For-profit competition is now as affordable due to overbuilding
– Vacancies in 50% to 65% of median income units
– Decreasing market rents in relation to regulated housing rents
– Rents not increasing with operating costs
– Costs of reporting requirements increases
– Turnover repair and replacement costs increasing
– Maintenance costs at crises level
– Increased cost of food services and staff for supportive housing program
– Marketing plan not developed or executed
– Partner agency costs for service delivery are increasing
– Support services—social workers not available
– Property taxes increasing off the chart
– Cannot rent 1 bedrooms
– High pool maintenance and operating costs
– Inadequate use of social marketing
– No preventative maintenance system
– Turnovers take 30 days
– No computer software
– Background screening not complete

REAL ESTATE PERFORMANCE STANDARDS

Operations

1. Expenses to Income, Total PUPA
2. Accounts Payable—Total, 60-day, 90-day
3. Occupancy Rate—%
4. Rent Collection—%
5. Eviction Timing
6. Turnaround Time
7. Work Order Systems—Time to respond
8. Energy Conservation Plan
9. Management Plan
10. Tenant Satisfaction
11. Turnover Rate
12. Operating Reserves—Balance
13. Reporting to Investors/Lenders/Regulators

Asset Preservation

1. Replacement Reserves—Balance/Monthly
2. Preventative Maintenance—Program
3. Disposition and Refinancing—Plan

Resident Relations & Services

1. Newsletter/Blog
2. # of police calls per month
3. Meeting Participation
4. Employment %
5. Savings Club
6. Day Care
7. Transportation

Management Considerations

1. Proforma vs. Current Rent
2. Insurance Assessment
3. Disaster Planning
4. Budget

Property Specific

1. Your choice
2. Participation in recycling program
3. Participation in healthy homes program
4. Participation in energy management program
5. Reduction in water use.
6. Reduction in heating and cooling costs
7. Participation in after school program

MY PROPERTY BENCHMARKS

Address_____ **Date** _____

	BEST PRACTICE	20____-20____ PERFORMANCE
OPERATIONS		
1a. Expenses to Income	Income exceeds all cash expenses including reserves	
1b. Total Operating Cost PUPA	75% of area	
2. Accounts Payable	Bills paid 100% within 60 days	
	85% within 30 days	
3. Occupancy Rate	95%	
4. Rent Collection	95% Tenant 100% Subsidy	
5. Eviction Timing	Within 5 days of legal date _____	
6. Turnaround Time	80%—3-5 business days 20%—10-15 business days	
7. Work Order Systems		
- Emergency	24 hours	
- Vacancy Refurbishment	3-15 business days	
- Preventative	90% within 2 weeks of schedule	
- Planned	Within 5 days of schedule	
-Tenant Requests	Within 3-7 business days	
8. Energy Conservation	Annual consumption/cost analysis	
9. Management Plan	Updated annually	
10. Tenant Satisfaction	Annual tenant satisfaction surveys	
11. Turnover Rate	Less than 20%	
12. Operating Reserves	10-25% per your of annual operating budget	
13. Reporting to Investors/ Lenders/Regulators	Within 5 days of reporting deadlines	
14.		

	BEST PRACTICE	20____-20____ PERFORMANCE
ASSET PRESERVATION		
1. Replacement Reserves	- Sufficient reserves to cover next major expense per CNA	
	- CNA updated every 5 years	
	- RR balance per CNA	
	- RR annual deposit $	
2. *Maintenance*		
- Unit Inspections	Annual unit inspections	
- Preventative Maintenance	Preventative maintenance plan	
- % Tenant Maintenance	Less than 20% of total	
- Maintenance Budget PUPA	Between $3,800 & $7,000	
3. Disposition and Refinancing Plan	Disposition and/or refinancing plan in place	
*4.		
RESIDENT RELATIONS & SERVICES		
Newsletter/Blog	Monthly distribution	
# of police calls per month	Under 1 per 100 units/week	
Meeting Participation	20% or 90% of invited	
Employment %	Increasing	
Savings Club	96% achievement of goal	
Day Care	80% of max capacity	
Transportation	2 times/week	
*8.		
*9.		
MANAGEMENT		
1. Proforma vs. Current Rent	1.0 or higher	
2. Insurance Assessment	Annual review	
3. Disaster Planning	Fire drill, disaster plan, annual review	
4. Budget	+/—4% annual	
*5.		

*Blank fields are for your property-specific performance standards

EXAMPLE
PROPERTY PERFORMANCE

Project: 12 Hopkins Street   **Date:** 06/04

	INDUSTRY STANDARD	2003-2004 PERFORMANCE	X
OPERATIONS			
1a. Expenses to Income	Income exceeds all expenses including reserves	X + 2000	
1b. Total Operating Cost PUPA	75% of area		
2. Accounts Payable	Bills paid 100% within 60 days	X	
	85% within 30 days	X	
3. Occupancy Rate	95%	98%	
4. Rent Collection	95% Tenant	99%	
	100% Subsidy	100%	
5. Eviction Timing	Within 5 days of legal date		
6. Turnaround Time	90%—3-10 business days	80%—10 days	
	10%—10-15 business days	X	
7. Work Order Systems			
- Emergency	24 hours	X	
- Vacancy Refurbishment	3-15 business days	X	
- Preventative	Within 2 weeks of schedule	X	
- Planned	Within 5 days of schedule	X	
- Tenant Requests	3-7 business days	X	
8. Energy Conservation	Annual consumption/cost analysis	X	
9. Management Plan	Updated annually	X	
10. Tenant Satisfaction	Annual tenant satisfaction surveys	Every other year	
11. Turnover Rate	Less than 10%	12%	

12. Operating Reserves	10-25% per your of annual operating budget	6%	
13. Reporting to Investors/ Lenders/Regulators	Within 5 days of reporting deadlines	X	

	INDUSTRY STANDARD	**2003-2004 PERFORMANCE**	**X**
ASSET PRESERVATION			
1. Replacement Reserves	Sufficient reserves to cover next major problem	No/short $42,000	
	CNA updated every 5 years	X	
	RR balance per CNA	X	
	RR being funded	X	
2. Maintenance Unit Inspections	Annual unit inspections	X	
Preventative Maintenance	Preventative maintenance plan	X	
% Tenant Maintenance	Less than 20% of total	24%	
Total Maintenance Budget PUPA	Between $3,800 & $7,000	$4,200	
3. Disposition and Refinancing	Disposition and/or plan in place	X	
SITE SPECIFIC	GOAL		
1. Proforma vs. current rent	1.0 or higher	1.06	
2. Financial education	12%/year	15% in 2003	

Chapter 4

ASSET MANAGEMENT HANDBOOK

CAPITAL NEEDS & LIFE CYCLE COSTS

Theme: Your perspectives of reality must be verified with objective measures.

Learning Objectives:

- To identify long-lasting materials

- To advocate early design decisions

- To identify lifecycle cost factors

- To recognize the pros and cons of 15 versus 50 year components

Essential Vocabulary:
— Life Cycle Cost
— Capital Improvements
— Life Expectancy
— Initial Cost
— Associated Cost
— Operating Cost

Assumed Experience: High School Algebra

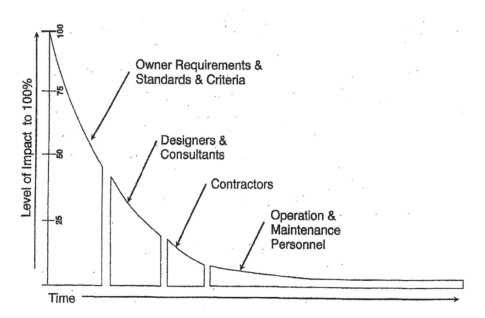

EARLY DECISIONS CREATE TODAY'S CONDITIONS

Early design and budget decisions are responsible for almost all of the reality that your maintenance personnel address today. Nonexistent or inaccurate life cycle cost analysis has created may properties that cannot last 15 years as affordable rental housing. Short term underwriting and design is fine in for-profit projects. When the affordability period is 20 to 40 years, the owner must plan to survive.

A LIFETIME OF CAPITAL IMPROVEMENTS
50 Years for a 1,300 SF Frame Home

History	% Initial Cost vs. % Value	Major Maintenance	Capital Replacement	Capital Improvement
Initial Construction Year 0: 1952 Min Wage: $.32 Rent: $45 Value: $4,600	N/A			Construction of 1,100 SF, 3-bed, 1 bath, oak floor, plaster walls, ceramic bath, wood cabinets, space heat, wood S.G. windows **Cost—$4,600**
Minor Improvements Year 20: 1972 Min Wage: $.75 Rent: $175 Value: $23,000	91% 17%		- Reroof - Aluminum siding - **Cost—$1,800**	- Block up foundation - Add laundry hookups - Add rear porch - **Cost—$2,300**
1st Modernization Year 35: 1987 **Min Wage: $1.90** Rent: $450 Value: $42,000	126% 14%	- Sand floors - Paint & patch - Replace countertop - Replace steps - **Cost—$1,800**		- Add central heat/AC - Upgrade electric service & panel - Add alum storms - Add attic insulation - **Cost—$4,000**
Minor Renovation Year 46: 1998 Min Wage: $3.85 Rent: $450 Value: $58,000	84% 6.7%		- Reroof - Replace vanity and tub surround - **Cost—$2,700**	- Add driveway apron - **Cost—$1,200**

Substantial Rehab		- Sand and	- Replace	- Add 2nd bath
Year 52: 2004		refinish floors	windows w/	- Add dishwasher
Min Wage: $5.35	1,280%	- Patch paint	PVC, DG	- Add cable
Rent: $650	47%	- Cost—$3,400	- Replace	wiring
Value: $125,000			plumbing	- Add wall
			Replace siding	insulation
			- Replace kitchen	- Add GFCI,
			- Replace bath	smoke detector
			- Rebuild porch	- Add 8' of closet
			- Cost—$19,500	- Remove 3 doors
				- Cost—$36,000
50 Year Totals		$5,200	$24,000	43,500
$72,700		15.8 times original *purchase* 58% of current value in capital repairs and maintenance		

15 Times Initial Purchase. In this real, single-family dwelling, $72,000 in maintenance, improvements and replacements were required in its first 50 years. That is 15.8 times the initial purchase price of $4,600. It still offers equity for the current owners as the property is worth approximately 40% more than the total investment. Pure, simple, real examples like these make it apparent that reserves of 1% of the initial construction cost will never be sufficient to adequately maintain a living dwelling.

DESIGN STANDARDS CONSIDERATIONS

THE 50+ YEAR PRODUCTS
(Still in service—2012)

- Ceramic tile set in 2" of concrete

- 2" thick pine front door

- All solid core interior doors

- Copper wiring

- Solid wood framing in walls, floors, roof

- Plaster on cement lathe walls

- Oak floors

- Masonry fireplace

- Cast iron and enamel tubs

THE 50-YEAR PRODUCTS
(Replaced at 50-Year Mark)

- Wood, double-hung, single-glazed windows

- Plumbing supply & waste lines (galvanized)

- Solid wood kitchen cabinets (market amenity)

- Stainless steel kitchen sink (for style upgrade)

- Exterior fascia

- Rear porch deck

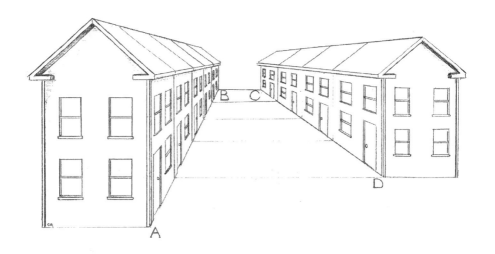

OPINIONS VERSUS REALITY

Many designers and operators have opinions about the cost, maintenance, and effectiveness of various components. This is especially true of green and energy investments. Just like the perception that line A-B is longer than line D-C, until you do the math with objective measurements, it is difficult to come to an accurate and scientifically correct opinion. In general, advocates minimize component cost and maximize their benefit. As a nonprofit property owner, you should always err in exactly the opposite way. You should maximize the potential cost and minimize the benefit. If it still works, use it all day long.

Estimated Life Expectancies of Systems and Components in Rental Property
(with normal maintenance)

Item	Life Expectancy in Years (Suggested Life)
Roofs	
___ fiberglass asphalt shingles	18-35 (30)
___ wood shingles	10-20
___ wood shakes	20-40
___ tile/terra-cotta tiles	40-60 (50)
___ slate shingles	50-100 (75)
___ metal roofing	20-60 plus
___ roll roofing	10-16
___ 5 ply/built-up roofs	18-35 (28)
___ asbestos-cement shingles	40-60 (50)
___ single-ply membrane	15-25 (25)
Chimneys	
___ masonry with clay liner	60-100
___ masonry without a liner	30-50
___ metal chimneys	10-20
___ pointing up (repair joints)	20-40 (25)
Gutters	
___ seamless aluminum	15-30 (25)
___ copper	40 plus
___ vinyl	10-20
___ downspout drywell	10-15
Siding	
___ wood boards	30 years to life of the building
___ wood shingles and shakes	20-40
___ hardboard (masonite)	10-20

___ stucco—3 coat	Life of the building
___ brick, block and stone	Life of the building
___ repoint brick 40 years to	life of the building
___ aluminum and steel 40 years to	life of the building
___ vinyl 40 years to	life of the building
___ asphalt shingles	30-40
___ fiber-cement shingles	Life of the building

Trim

___ wood trim	20-life of building
___ metal trim	Life of building
___ vinyl trim	30-life of building

Decks/Porches

___ composite material	20-25 (20)
___ treated wood	20-30 plus (25)

Shutters

___ wood	20
___ metal	20-40
___ plastic/vinyl	40 plus
___ aluminum	40 plus

Windows and Doors

___ vinyl, double hung	40-65 (40)
___ wood, double-hung windows	40-life of building
___ window glazing	6-14
___ steel casement windows	30-40
___ jalousie windows	25-40
___ aluminum storm windows	20-40
___ aluminum & glass entrance door	25-35 (30)
___ screen doors (wood)	5-8
___ storm doors (alum)	10-15
___ interior doors (molded)	12-16
___ garage doors	20-30

Exterior Painting

___ wood	5-7
___ brick	5
___ aluminum	10-12
___ trim	5-7

Exterior Staining

___ wood	5-10

Driveways

___ asphalt	16-35
___ concrete	30-45
___ gravel	10-20

Swimming Pools

___ pool shell	15-25
___ pool filter	3-5
___ pool heater	4-7
___ pool liner	8-12
___ above-ground pool	7-10

Other Exterior Items

___ sprinkler system	15-25 (18)
___ wood fence (untreated)	7-12
___ pressure-treated fence	30 plus
___ concrete patio	15-25
___ tennis court	20-40
___ chain link fence	30 plus
___ rescue fire escape	20-35 (30)

Heating and Cooling

___ forced air furnaces	18-25 (22)
___ steel boilers	15-25

___ cast-iron boilers	30-50
___ heat pump compressors	8-15 (10)
___ air conditioning system	15-25 (20)
___ air-conditioning compressor	8-12
___ gas chiller	10-15
___ window air-conditioning unit	7-18 (14)
___ wall air-conditioning unit	10-20
___ radiant heat coils	15-25
___ zone valves	3-5
___ electric baseboard	15 plus
___ wall convector heater	15 plus
___ air-to-air heat exchanger	15 plus
___ electronic air cleaner	10-15
___ expansion tank	30 plus
___ relief valves	20 plus
___ gas thermocouple	10-20
___ oil tank	30-40
___ buried oil tank	15-25
___ thermostat	20 plus
___ combustion chamber	10-15
___ stack relay	10-20
___ flame-retention burner	10-20
___ circulator pump	10-15
___ condensate pump	5-10
___ humidifier	2-10
___ heat exchanger	5-30
___ galvanized heat ducts	50-70
___ fiberglass heat ducts	40-60
___ warm-air blowers	10-15
___ solid-fuel stove	10-15
___ motors and pumps	5-10
___ fan relay	10-20
___ humidistat	5-10
___ radiator valve	20 plus
___ barometric damper	30 plus
___ flue pipes	10-15

Plumbing

____ copper water pipes	50-60
____ plastic water pipes	35-50
____ cast-iron drains	50 plus
____ galvanized pipe drains	30-50
____ plastic drains	50 plus
____ metal shower pan	8-10
____ plastic shower pan	20-40
____ septic leaching fields	18-22
____ submersible well pump	10
____ pressure tank	20 plus
____ sump pump	5-7
____ commode	20-25 (20)
____ faucet	6-12
____ shower valve	8-15 (10)

Domestic Hot Water

____ gas-fired hot-water tank	6-12 (10)
____ oil-fired hot-water tank	10-12
____ electric hot-water tank	11-17 (15)
____ internal tankless coils	10-15 plus
____ external tankless unit	10-20 plus
____ booster tank	10-20 plus

Electrical

____ fixtures	17-40 (22)
____ wiring (copper and aluminum)	Life of house
____ circuit breaker panel	30-40
____ circuit breakers	25-35
____ electric fixtures	20-30
____ doorbell and chimes	7-12
____ smoke detector	10-17 (15)

Ventilation

___ kitchen exhaust fan	12-17
___ bathroom exhaust fan	10-15
___ paddle fan	5-30
___ attic roof fan	10-20
___ attic gable fan	10-20
___ ridge, soffit and gable vents	Life of the house

Appliances & Cabinets

___ kitchen cabinets	20-40 (36)
___ bathroom vanities	7-40 (22)
___ ranges (electric)	10-22 (16)
___ ranges (gas)	12-27 (19)
___ ovens	15-25
___ microwave oven	10
___ refrigerators	10-18 (14)
___ disposals	8-12 (10)
___ trash compactors	5-12
___ dishwashers	7-14 (10)
___ dryer	11-17 (13)
___ washing machine	7-16 (12)
___ instant hot water unit	5-10
___ dehumidifier	5-12 (8)
___ humidifier	5-15 (9)

Floors

___ oak	125
___ pine	55
___ slate, quarry, flagstone	40-60
___ ceramic tile	40 plus
___ resilient (tile)	6-20 (18)
___ terrazzo	Life of the building
___ carpeting	2-16 (8)
___ vinyl sheetgoods	7-20 (18)

LIFE CYCLE COST ELEMENTS

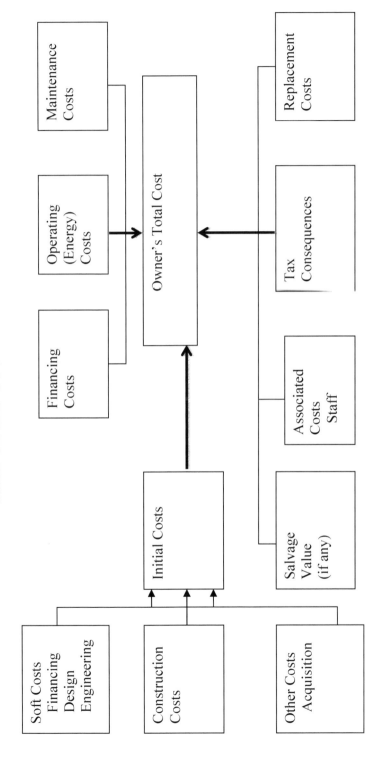

Life Cycle Costs (LCC)

LCC identifies the total building costs over an extended time period. When in-depth LCC is applied, the model is comprised of the following elements:

Initial Costs are the original construction, acquisition, and development costs of the structure. This includes the hard costs and change orders along with design fees, financing fees and rent-up costs. Initial cost is made up of three categories. 1) soft costs; 2) construction hard costs, and 3) all other costs of the acquisition.

Financing Costs reflect the mortgage interest payments, rate and amortization schedule. A true value of money rather than actual property interest rate, i.e. 6% versus 1% is factored.

Operating Costs are the lifetime energy costs of the subcomponent or structure. For example: How much water does it use? How much electricity does it use? Some components can pay for themselves by selling power back to the grid

Maintenance Costs captures both direct payroll and contracted services to create a maintenance program assuming adequate preventative maintenance to achieve the design life.

Replacement Costs are the future one-time costs to remove and replace the current component with a modern equivalent.

Tax Consequences measures the cost impact of the tax laws. These costs should be continually updated as tax laws change; for example, investment tax credits are available for alternative energy systems, depreciation rates and periods can be used, and different depreciation recapture rules must be applied.

Associated Costs adds items such as insurance, additional vacancy, decreased income, additional time, and staffing costs to maintain ongoing operations. Two daycare centers have similar initial costs. One daycare center can service 106 clients per day with a total staff of 10 people; the other center requires a staff of 14 to care for the same number of clients.

The design that uses less staff is more cost effective. In-depth LCC analysis calculates this cost difference.

As a second example of associated costs, there are two building renovation options with identical costs. One option requires relocating people out of each unit for two months; the other scenario could be accomplished during non-working hours. In LCC, the cost of relocation and net loss of rents would be quantified.

The cost impact of insurance was illustrated by a recent study of a lead hazard reduction program. All costs were comparable, but one system had a lower annual insurance premium. In this case, the present worth of the annual insurance rates was used for each alternative in the LCC.

Salvage Value represents the economic value, if any, of components at the end of the life cycle period. The value is positive if it has residual economic value, and negative if additional costs, such as extensive demolition of a swimming pool, are required.

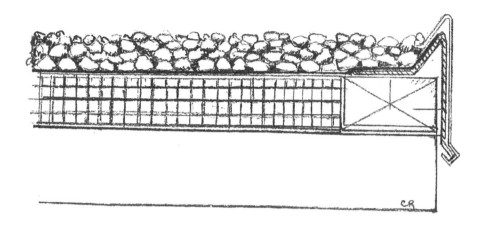

BUY SMART

The fully ballasted Elastomeric roof over 4" of insulation board may cost more in the initial construction but it wins over BUR in the long run. The additional cost is repaid in a 6 year longer estimated life and a 12% reduction in heat and cooling loss.

Chapter 5

ASSET MANAGEMENT HANDBOOK

CNA POLICIES

Theme: Great policy is the starting point for effective and efficient procedures.

Learning Objectives:
- Identify 8 policies and their options for owners
- Identify 3 rules of thumb
- Select a rational inflation rate

Essential Vocabulary:
— Sum of digits
— Replacement index
— Future standards
— Refinance cycle
— Renovation style

Assumed Experience: Six months in real estate, property management, banking or development industry or two years of higher education

BUILD A CENTRAL POLICY TEAM

In all areas of system development, decisions evolve into policies and procedures that are implemented by practices carried out with tools and documents.

Stephen Covey's *The 7 Habits of Highly Effective People* has become ensconced in platinum as some of the ultimate business advice. His second point was "Begin with the end in mind." In most of the dysfunctional organizations I've been privileged to work with, this rule was overlooked from the start. The policy makers were powerful, well educated, experienced in administration but had no solid idea what the end goal was implementing.

Of course, I've also seen the opposite extreme, a serious case of "paralysis by analysis." Every minute decision was run through a gauntlet of both risk and end point analysis with so many variables, assumptions and unknowns that it stagnates the decision process. The end result is that the search for perfection (which somebody else has said many times) is the "enemy of the good".

Experience is necessary. There are 8 significant policies that must be evaluated and applied in portfolio asset management and approximately 50 procedures to follow up with implementing those policies. It is very important that at least one major contributor on the policy team be knowledgeable in asset management, long-term ownership and preservation of the type of property you are considering.

I have a lot of background in real estate development and when I see policymakers strike out on their own, it reminds me of a bunch of adolescents deciding to wire a house. And then becoming frustrated and surprised that there are requirements called the code, minimum standards, wire size, type of electrical boxes, and air sealing requirements which even a beginning electrician understands.

But policymakers are usually bold, some aggressive, successful, intelligent and this do-it-yourself type attitude can be quite pervasive. I suggest that everyone recognize what they know and what they don't know. During the time period when you are developing your asset management policies, do it in consultation with an experienced asset manager. Once you've completed your policies, the procedures are more cut and dry. They are based on: efficiency, the tools that you have, and the knowledge and skill base of the team carrying out the policy.

ESSENTIAL CNA POLICY DECISIONS

#1 What method shall we use to calculate our replacement reserve?

_____

#2 What rate of inflation shall we assume? _____

#3 What is our renovation style?

_____

_____

#4 How much deferred and unfunded maintenance, repairs and replacements will we allow?

_____   _____

_____

#5 How will we grade and analyze the remaining economic life of our building parts?

_____

_____

#6 What is our required precision in evaluating remaining economic life?

_____

_____

#7 How shall we incorporate, known and projected future standards into our CNA?

_____

_____

#8 What is a capital replacement and what is maintenance?

_____

_____

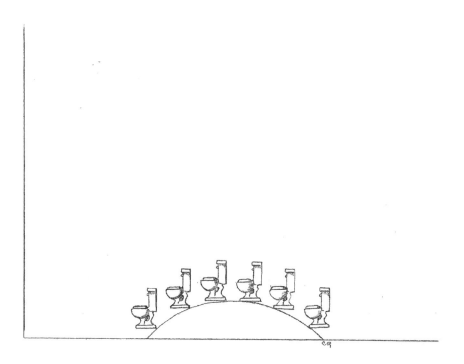

REPLACEMENT STYLE

Your renovation policy requires you to decide how you are going to time the reworking of the building. It is very common for plumbing and electrical fixtures to be replaced along a 7-year curve versus all at once. Instead of needing 70 toilets in Year 1 of their expected life, many types of equipment can be spread out over various curves. The spreadsheet allows you to pick 3 styles: all at once, over 3 years, or over a 7 year curve. Other items that are normally replaced on a curve include: stoves, refrigerators, maybe window or through the wall air conditioners. Whole kitchen and bath replacements are completed over time, especially to avoid temporary relocation.

POLICY OPTION: METHOD OF CALCULATION

Policy Question #1: What method shall we use to calculate our replacement reserve?

Calculate Based on Total Replacement Cost and One of the Following Formulas:

Rules of Thumb:

1. Straight-line percentage of total development cost

2. Sum-of-digits

3. Replacement index

Evaluation of Property Condition

1. Life cycle costs

Advantages

_____

_____

_____

Concerns

_____

_____

_____

Recommendations

_____

_____

_____

STRAIGHT-LINE CALCULATIONS

A simple straight-line projection of a building with a fifty-year life declines at the rate of two percent a year. Although a crude rule of thumb, this approach would require that two percent of a building's replacement value be set aside each year.

FORMULA:

$$\frac{100}{\text{Life of Building}} = \% \text{ depreciation per year}$$

Annual % Deprecation x Development Cost = Annual Replacement Reserve

EXAMPLE:

$$\frac{100}{40 \text{ Year Life}} = 2.5\% \text{ Annual Depreciation}$$

2.5% x ($95,000/unit x 26 units)
2.5% x ($2,470,000)

= $61,750 per year/per project

or

$2,375 PUPA

or

$198 PUPM

50-YEAR SUM-OF-THE-DIGITS CALCULATIONS

A building with an expected fifty-year life cycle is "aged" so that at the end of fifty years, it reaches its full replacement value. The adjusted formula is equal to the building age divided by 1275 (where 1275 equals the sum of $1 + 2 + 3 + 4 + \ldots 49 + 50 = 1275$). This formula will eventually generate almost four percent a year (50/1275) of its current replacement value. In this formula, older buildings require more replacement reserves than newer buildings.

Factors can forecast that at the end of a building's life, 2/3, 3/4, or 100 percent of the building value (BV) requires replacement. Variables used in the calculation are: the building age and current replacement value for an equivalent building.

FORMULA:

Annual Replacement Reserve = 2/3 Building Value x Building Age/1275

Where:

Annual Replacement Reserve = the funding which should be allocated annually

   2/3 = The building replacement percentage or .66
   BV = The building value
   BA = The building age as corrected for either partial or total building
        replacement
   1275 = The age-weighting constant based on a 50-year life

EXAMPLE:

An unrenovated, 26-unit building constructed in 1998 at a current (2012) replacement cost of $2,912,000 or $112,000 per unit

Annual Allowance   = 2/3 BV x BA/1275

2012 Allowance   = .66 $2,912,000 x 14/1275
                           = $1,921,920 x .010
                           = $19,219 per project per annum

                           $739 PUPA this year and increasing every year

                           $61 PUPM

REPLACEMENT INDEX CALCULATIONS

A more refined approach than formulas involves the use of replacement cycles for renewing building components and systems to produce a replacement index. The index is expressed as a percent value equivalent to the portion of a building that must be replacement annually and includes the following factors:

Building Type—subsystems and associated costs vary widely across the range of building types, i.e. hospitals and townhouses.

Date of Construction—the original date of construction and date of major additions and renovations affect renewal funding needs.

Building subsystems—the quantity and quality of installed subsystems within a facility will determine replacement requirements.

Subsystem life cycles—predictable life of a subsystem will determine when future replacement requirements will occur.

Subsystem cost—unit replacement cost for subsystems effect future requirements.

A replacement index for the purposes of computing an annual renewal allowance for a facility uses the following steps:

1. Define building systems
2. Estimate each system costs
3. Calculate system costs as percentage of total construction cost
4. Estimate system replacement life
5. Calculate replacement index

A sample calculation of a replacement index for a low-rise (one to four story) building follows the steps outlined below.

STEP ONE—DEFINE BUILDING SYSTEMS

The building components outlined in Column One of the example are those used in *Means Square Foot Costs* for a similar building type. A uniform listing of building components should be used for consistency in the factors for developing replacement indexes for various building types.

STEPS TWO AND THREE—ESTIMATE SYSTEM COSTS AND SYSTEM PERCENT OF TOTAL CONSTRUCTION

Building component costs are obtained from *Means Square Foot Costs* for a similar building type. The percent of total construction is calculated by dividing the cost of each component into the total project cost.

STEP FOUR—ESTIMATE SYSTEM LIFE CYCLE

Various sources provide the average number of years before replacement or major repairs are required, to estimate the life of a component. A secondary set of calculations may be required for a facility with a major renovation.

STEP FIVE—CALCULATE REPLACEMENT INDEX

The final step in the calculation is to divide the "Percent of Total Construction" (Column 3) by the "System Replacement Life" (Column 4) to produce a "Replacement Index" percentage for each component (Column 5). The total of the component indexes results in a replacement index or annual replacement allowance of 2.90 percent of the current replacement value of the building.

Analyses using this procedure must be performed for different building types. An overall summary replacement index may be developed for an organization's portfolio. This final amount provides a rough guide for annual capital budgeting of repair and replacement needs.

EXAMPLE

REPLACEMENT INDEX FOR A ONE TO FOUR STORY APARTMENT BUILDING

Building Component	Development Cost per Square Foot	Percent of Total Development Cost	System Replacement Life	Replacement Index = % per Year of Total
1. Foundations	$ 2.36	2.25	100	.023
2. Substructure	1.70	1.61	100	.016
3. Superstructure	11.46	10.90	100	.109
4. Exterior Closure	10.44	9.93	50	.199
5. Roofing	1.80	1.71	15	.114
6. Int. Construction	23.76	22.61	20	1.130
7. Conveying	3.98	3.79	25	.152
8. Mechanical	17.48	16.63	25	.665
9. Electrical	12.44	11.84	40	.296
10. Equipment				
11. Spec. Construction				
12. Site Work				
General Conditions (15%) Arch Fees (7%)	$12.82 $ 6.86	12.20 6.53	50	.375
TOTAL BUILDING COST	$105.10	100		

Replacement Index = 3.27% of $105.10/SF

Annual Need: 920 SF Unit = $3.44 x 920 = $3,164 or $263/month

RULE OF THUMB CALCULATIONS
WORKSHEET #1

Total Development Cost $_____

Year Reconstructed _____

Straight Line

        _____
        _____
        _____
        _____

50-Year Sum of Digits

        _____
        _____
        _____
        _____

Replacement Index:

        _____
        _____
        _____
        _____

POLICY OPTION: INFLATION RATE

Policy Question #2: What rate of inflation shall we assume?

1. Replace component depreciation only.

2. Replace @ 5% inflation for the component.

3. Replace @ Construction Cost Index rate for last 20 years or _____%.

Advantages

_____

_____

_____

Concerns

_____

_____

_____

Recommendations

_____

_____

_____

PLAN ONE
COVER DEPRECIATION

REFRIGERATOR—10 YEAR LIFE—$575 COST

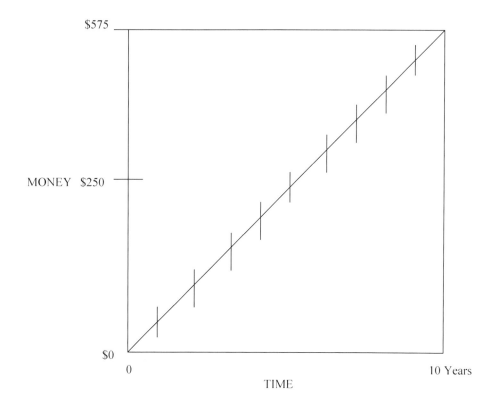

Plan—$57.50/Year or $4.80/Month Per Refrigerator

To replace our $575 refrigerator, we have dutifully put away $4.80 a month for 10 years. With the minimal interest we have earned we have successfully saved $575 and are now ready to go to market to buy our new refrigerators for each and every unit.

Why will we be short over 100%?

NEW JERSEY 2012
CURRENT UNIT COSTS PER MEANS COST DATA
Labor, Material, Overhead, Profit and Contingency

Appliances ( )		**My Cost**	*P.C.P.A.
Kitchen cabinet, LF up & down	$ 132	$_____	$_____
Reface cabinets LF	65	$_____	$_____
Replace countertop LF	42	$_____	$_____
Stoves electric 30"	335	$_____	$_____
gas	360	$_____	$_____
Refrigerator 20 CF side/side	950	$_____	$_____
Dishwasher 2 cycle	485	$_____	$_____
Garbage disposal 1/2 HP	127	$_____	$_____
Washer 3 cycle	800	$_____	$_____
Dryer 2 cycle	715	$_____	$_____
Window A/C unit 12,000 BTU	485	$_____	$_____
Range Hood	272	$_____	$_____

Flooring (_____% increase)

Carpet 22 oz nylon SF	1.82	$_____	$_____
Common area comm. carpet 38 oz SF	4.06	$_____	$_____
Office commercial carpet tiles SF	3.27	$_____	$_____
Vinyl sheet goods SF	3.74	$_____	$_____

Roofing (_____% increase)

Asphalt shingles SF	2.25	$_____	$_____
Built-up 3 ply SF	3.10	$_____	$_____
Single ply—Elastomeric SF	4.74	$_____	$_____

HVAC (_____% increase)
Individual/Furnace

Gas 60 MBH Ea	1,920	$_____	$_____
Electric 34 MBH Ea	745	$_____	$_____

AC—Residential Unit

Heat pump Ea   6,200 $_____ $_____

*P.C.P.A. = Per Component Per Annum

	My Cost	**P.C.P.A.**
Plumbing Fixtures (_____% increase) Ea		
Gas water heater 30 gal	780	$_____	$_____
Electric water heater 40 gal	505	$_____	$_____
Kitchen faucets, single lever	96	$_____	$_____
Lavatory faucets, single lever	55	$_____	$_____
Vanity	385	$_____	$_____
Tub diverters	275	$_____	$_____
Toilets	293	$_____·_____	$_____
Toilet mechanism	27	$_____	$_____
Tub and surround	900	$_____	$_____
Accessory set	65	$_____	$_____
Electric Fixtures (_____% increase) Ea		
GFCI ea	26	$_____	$_____
Bath fans	92	$_____	$_____
Kitchen fans	158	$_____	$_____
Light fixtures	46	$_____	$_____
Thermostat ea	76	$_____	$_____
Paving (_____% increase)		
Retopping SY	1.02	$_____	$_____
Replace SY	15.72	$_____	$_____
Painting (_____% increase)		
Prep and paint each room	390	$_____	$_____

KITCHEN DEPRECIATION EXERCISE

REPLACEMENT COST

Resurface (18-year) 8 LF Cabinets @ $_____ = $_____

Replace (27-year) 8 LF Cabinets @ $_____ = $_____

Replace 10 LF Countertop @ $_____   = $_____

Replace 1 Gas Stove @ $_____   = $_____

Replace 1 Refrigerator @ $_____   = $_____

Replace 100 SF Vinyl Sheetgoods @ $_____ = $_____

Replace 1 Kitchen Faucet @ $_____   = $_____

Replace 1 Range Hood @ $_____   = $_____

Replace 2 GFI's @ $_____   = $_____

Repaint and Patch 1 Room @ $_____   = $_____

Total Replacement Cost—27 year $_____

Total Replacement Cost—18 year $_____

@ 27 Year Life
Maximum Time from Annual Need $_____ PUPA

@ 18 Year Life
Recommended Time from Annual Need $_____ PUPA

(PUPA = Per Unit Per Annum)

BATHROOM DEPRECIATION EXERCISE

REPLACEMENT COST

Replace 1 Commode @ $_____   = $_____

Replace Tub & Surround @ $_____   = $_____

Replace 1 Vanity @ $_____   = $_____

Replace 1 Single Lever Faucet @ $_____   = $_____

Replace 60 SF Vinyl Sheetgoods @ $_____ = $_____

Replace 1 Tub Diverter @ $_____   = $_____

Replace 1 Bathroom Fan @ $_____   = $_____

Replace 1 GFI @ $_____   = $_____

Replace Accessories 1 @ $_____   = $_____

Replace 1 Light Fixture @ $_____   = $_____

Repaint and Patch 1 Room @ $_____   = $_____

Total Replacement Cost—27 year $_____

Total Replacement Cost—18 year $_____

@ 27 Year Life
Maximum Time from Annual Need $_____ PUPA

@ 18 Year Life
Recommended Time from Annual Need $_____ PUPA

(PUPA = Per Unit Per Annum)

REFRIGERATOR
REPLACEMENT COST ≠ DEPRECIATION COST

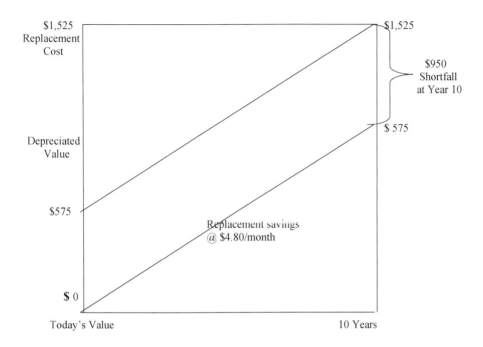

WHY SHORTFALL?

10 YEARS OF 5% INFLATION

DEPRECIATION USES HISTORIC COST
REPLACEMENT REQUIRES FUTURE VALUE

Having dutifully saved our $575, we are shattered to learn that the 10 year cost of the refrigerator has rapidly accelerated much faster than both our deposit to the replacement reserve and our insignificant earnings from interest. The combination of inflation and a head start based on $575 leaves us $950 short per refrigerator. And we thought we were doing so well. At least we have the money to replace the worst refrigerators. Partial replacement rewards the most abusive tenants while punishing the occupants who take care of our property. Maybe it's best to move the new refrigerators into the best cared for units and the used refrigerators into the abusive boxes. Difficult though, because it's all at turnover.

COVER DEPRECIATION AND FACTOR IN INFLATION @ 5% PER YEAR

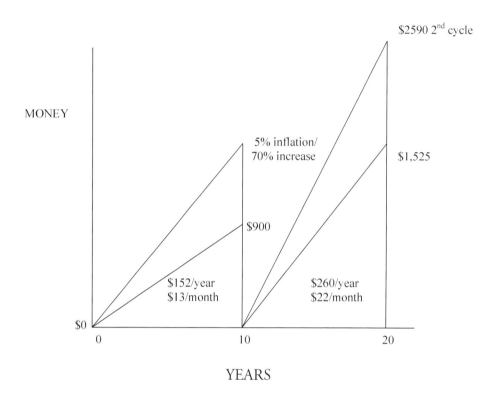

But without an increase in deposit = bankrupt replacement account.

So increase every replacement cycle period (10 years) to adjust for actual inflation rate.

CONSTRUCTION INDUSTRY
HISTORICAL COST INDEXES

Year	Historical Cost Index Jan 1 1993 = 100		Current Index Based on Jan 1 1999 = 100		Year	Historical Cost Index Jan 1 1993 = 100	Current Index Based on Jan 1, 1999 = 100		Year	Historical Cost Index Jan 1 1993 = 100	Current Index Based on Jan 1 1999 = 100	
	Est.	Actual	Est.	Act		Actual	Est	Act		Actual	Est	Act
2004		133			July 1984	82.2	70.4		July 1996	22.7	19.5	
2003		130	100.0									
2002		128.7										
2001		125.1										
2000		120.9			1983	80.2	68.9		1965	21.7	18.6	
1999		117.6			1981	70.0	60.1		1963	20.7	17.8	
1998		115.1	98.9		1980	62.9	54.0		1962	20.2	17.4	
1997		112.8	96.9		1979	57.8	49.7		1961	19.8	17.0	
1996		110.2	94.7		1978	53.5	46.0		1960	19.7	16.9	
1995		107.6	92.4		1977	49.5	42.5		1959	19.3	16.6	
1994		104.4	89.7		1976	46.9	40.3		1958	18.8	16.2	
1993		101.7	87.4		1975	44.8	38.5		1957	18.4	15.8	
1992		99.4	85.4		1974	41.1	35.6		1956	17.6	15.1	
1991		96.8	83.3		1973	37.7	32.4		1955	16.6	14.3	
1990		94.3	81.0		1972	34.8	29.9		1954	16.0	13.7	
1989		92.1	79.2		1971	32.1	27.6		1953	15.8	13.6	
1988		89.9	77.2		1970	28.7	24.7		1952	15.4	13.2	
1987		87.7	75.3		1969	26.9	23.1		1951	15.0	12.91	
1986		84.2	72.4		1968	24.9	21.4		1950	13.7	11.8	
1985		82.6	71.0		1967	23.5	20.2		1949	13.3	11.4	

10 Year Rate = _____ % (100-_____)

20 Year Rate = _____ % (100-_____)

1998-2004 _____ %

Source: R.S. Means *Repair & Remodeling Cost Data 2004*

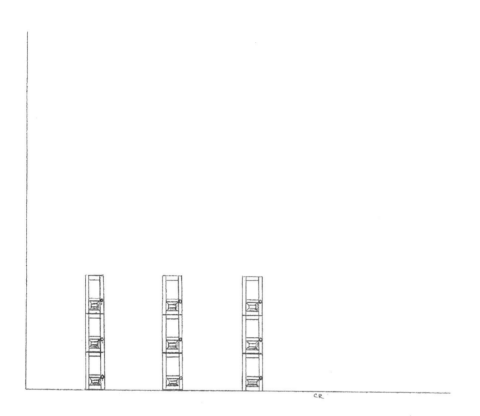

3 YEAR SPLITS

Fortunately not everything breaks down on exactly the same day according to the expected life table. Some components will have experienced a more demanding life and others will have been treated very well. Spreading out the capital expenditures needed to replace all of the items is very helpful. Maybe we can use a smaller subcontractor to work diligently for 3 years replacing 100 doors a year rather than replacing all 300 doors within the same 60 day period.

REPLACEMENT TIMING OPTIONS

Policy Question #3: What is our renovation style?

1. Simultaneous replacement of 100% for every component in every unit

---

1. Replacement at variable rates per system requirements

    A. 100%: roofing, paving, boilers, exterior paint, windows

    B. 3 year spread: 1/3 each year—roof, paint, flooring, doors

    C. Normal 7-Year Curve: basic appliances (stoves), ceramic tile

Advantages

Concerns

Recommendations

NOT ALL COMPONENTS BREAK AT THE SAME TIME

100% ONLY WORKS FOR "ONE TIME DEALS"

EG. ROOF, REPAVE PARKING, BOILER REPLACEMENT,
EXTERIOR PAINT OF ENTIRE PROJECT   }   100%

Your CNA spreadsheet can reflect 3 style options:

100%

One is that you are projecting that all of your funds will come in from refinancing and your replacement reserves will be used in conjunction with these monies for a one-time event. That means you have to have all of the money in the same place at the same time to do all of the repairs.

3-Year Splits

Let's say you have 200 units and they are in 16 buildings and you need to replace the roofs. You might schedule to do one-third of them in Year 1; one-third in Year 2, and one-third in Year 3. This spreads out the need for all of the money in one year as it is very clear that you have three years to execute the work.

The Normal Curve

Here you are looking at items that require replacement over a relatively long time period. We have chosen 7 years for our spreadsheet. In this we are looking at the breakdown of stoves, for example, although they might have a median life of 14 years, due to use and abuse and care, some will begin to require replacement as early as Year 10 while others will last as long as Year 17. By choosing this normal curve of failure, you can significantly stretch out the replacement reserve requirements.

Many practitioners will use the 7-year curve, but at a certain point, say Year 5, decide to finish replacing all of the units, maybe keeping some of the better used equipment as emergency replacements. We call this "chopping off" the replacement option.

REPLACEMENT AS THINGS WEAR OUT

FAILURE ALONG A *NORMAL* CURVE

100% OF GRAPH NOT ALWAYS VALID IN A 100-UNIT BUILDING
(USE .75 X TOTAL FOR APPLIANCES, CARPET)

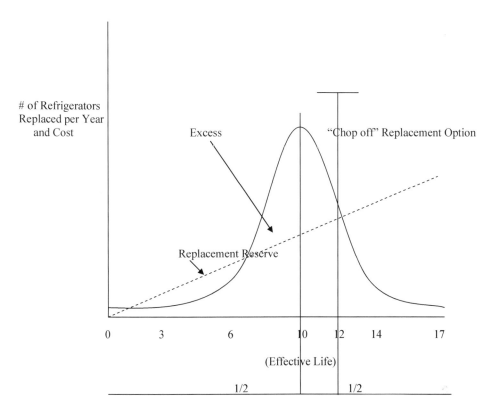

POLICY OPTION: WHEN TO REFINANCE

Policy Question #4: How much deferred and unfunded maintenance, repairs and replacements will we allow?

A. Only build reserves for problems during our "watch".

1. Refinance at 15 years
2. Refinance at 25 years
3. Refinance when reserve shortfall exceeds $500,000 or $1 million per CNA
4. Refinance at 40 years

B. Hold reserves for future owner/operators of permanently affordable housing.

Advantages

_____

_____

_____

Concerns

_____

_____

_____

Recommendations

_____

_____

_____

Chapter 6

ASSET MANAGEMENT HANDBOOK

FIELD EVALUATIONS & REPLACEMENT REQUIREMENTS

Theme:

It's not how old are you but how long are you going to last?

Learning Objectives:

- To evaluate different approaches to calculate remaining life

- To draft replacement reserve inspection policy

- To practice 3 quick and dirty annual reserve calculations

- To practice a field evaluation using the preformed spreadsheet

- To identify capital vs maintenance items

Essential Vocabulary:

— Value Engineering
— Remaining Economic life
— Mid Point Value
— Future Improvements
— Life Safety
— Healthy Homes Techniques
— Replacement Factor

THE OVERVIEW

CAPITAL REPLACEMENT FUNDING

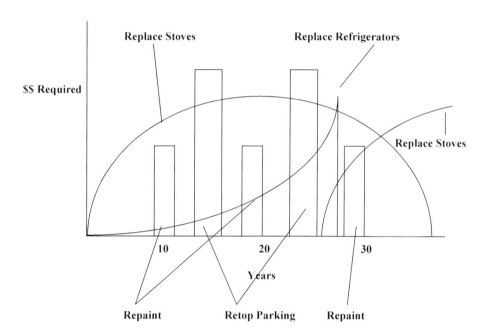

After analyzing the remaining life and its cost, the Excel spreadsheet can be used to depict graphs. The replacement factor you've selected will post the replacement items to the spreadsheet. Seven year normal curves for replacing the stoves over a 20-year period. An accelerating curve to replace 50% of refrigerators as they break down and then, at a certain point, the remaining 50%.

POLICY OPTION: REMAINING LIFE

Policy Question 5: How will we grade and analyze the remaining economic life of our building parts?

1. Remaining life per date installed using chart of typical life without inspection

2. Remaining life per field grading every 5 years

3. Remaining life per maintenance inspection and value engineering calculation

Advantages

_____

_____

_____

Concerns

_____

_____

_____

Recommendations

_____

_____

_____

VALUE ENGINEERING FOR REPLACEMENTS

Value engineering for the asset manager is a rational method of making cost-efficient choices between alternatives when upgrading, maintaining and installing system replacements. Value engineering determines how to maximize overall performance while minimizing costs. Building systems wear out in time; many deteriorate rapidly at the end. Maintenance of roofs, windows, mechanical systems, carpeting and paint finishes require more attention and more money each year they age. Value engineering calculations compare the annual maintenance costs for a particular system versus the cost of replacement alternatives.

Accelerating Maintenance Cost
For certain building systems that wear out, the annual operating costs increase each year. In determining the capital needs budget, it is necessary to calculate the escalating annual operating costs for a particular system. When replacement would result in overall lower costs or increased revenue, it makes the case for an immediate capital replacement.

Market Cost
Some choices do not affect operating costs directly but may result in increased marketability, for example, building colors. Pink ceramic tile and lime green halls have a negative impact on the marketability of the property, are difficult to maintain and affect the attitudes of both tenants and maintenance staff. In value engineering, these factors are identified, qualified and analyzed to inform rational decision.

Lighting—LED—The Way
Maintenance of common area and site lighting is an annual expense. The costs of relamping, the energy cost to operate the lights and the additional costs to cool the building from lighting loads are significant. Electric companies encourage efficient use of electric power by paying all or part of the cost for a building analysis. Some will finance a complete retrofit with high-efficiency LED fixtures. In this case, not only is there minimal cost for the capital improvement, but the following year's costs for both lighting and the related HVAC cooling costs will be lower.

Boilers, Furnaces & Air Conditioning—Replace Now

Making the choice between maintaining heating and cooling equipment and replacing it is an easy value engineering analysis. Older equipment is significantly less efficient than newer models and requires more care. To establish operating costs, annual repair and maintenance and annual fuel costs must be quantified. Maintenance and fuel costs are easily obtainable, and the comparative costs of equipment replacement, as well as the fuel and maintenance costs for new equipment, are simple to estimate using subcontractor proposals.

Equipment over 15 years old usually have operating efficiencies below 75% and new equipment has operating efficiencies above 90%—thus it is not difficult to calculate the operating savings and payback associated with replacement of older equipment.

An additional benefit of equipment replacement may be an increase in useable floor area. New equipment is considerably smaller than older equipment.

When contemplating removal of HVAC equipment, the costs of demolition and related asbestos removal, when present, must be added to the replacement cost.

Roofing

Over time, roofs wear and leak. Joints separate, membranes become worn or punctured and flashings corrode. Each year, the building's repair history can identify the costs of patching. The following factors are usually considered when evaluating the costs of maintaining a deteriorating roof:
— Annual repairs to fix leaks
— Ceiling repair
— Carpet replacement/cleaning
— Loss of rent due to perception of a poor quality building
— Increased energy costs resulting from wet insulation

The current annual operating costs can be compared to the costs for replacing the roof with various alternatives. For example, if the existing roof is B.U.R. and gravel, alternatives include EPDM, TPO, PVC. Energy saving from installing highly reflective roofing should also be considered.

Windows
The principal direct and indirect costs associated with window replacement are:
– Maintenance costs for painting, sash repair and caulking
– Energy loss from air leakage
– Energy losses resulting from single-pane glass
– Water damage to carpets, paint and plaster from leaking windows

When these costs are quantified and compared with improvements such as storm windows, interior glazing, new double-insulated glass in a variety of frame types including fiberglass and PVC, some rational choices can be made.

POLICY OPTION: FIELD GRADING ACCURACY

Policy Question 6: What is our required precision in evaluating economic life?

1. Life in 3 categories with midpoint value

2. Life in 5 categories with midpoint value

3. Life per operator's and asset manager's best aging estimate

Advantages

_____

_____

_____

Concerns

_____

_____

_____

Recommendations

_____

_____

_____

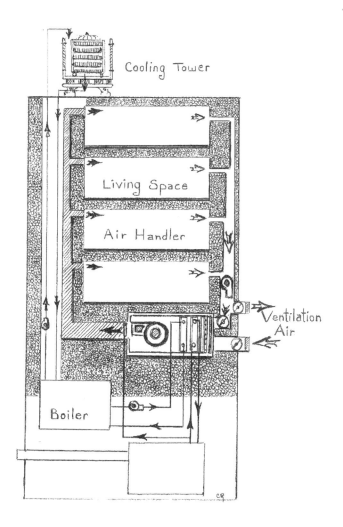

Cooling Tower

Living Space

Air Handler

Ventilation Air

Boiler

GET PROFESSIONAL HELP

Unless you know the components of a cooling tower, a boiler, and your make-up air with its sophisticated controls, do not age these mechanical systems. Seek out help from professionals. You should have maintenance subcontractors willing to provide you not only a proposal that identifies needs, but also current costs. Often the code will have changed significantly over the 20 or 30 years since the central equipment was installed. Entirely new systems are not only more energy efficient but required by governmental guidance.

CONDITION CATEGORIES

A. 3-TIERED SYSTEM—ABC

Under the ABC or 3-tiered system grades, a relatively inexperienced observer can sort the component system into one of three bins. The second step is to look up the typical life span of that item from the charts. That typical age is divided in thirds and the midpoint of each third is used as the remaining economic life of the component.

EXAMPLE

33.3%   12 year life

B condition   6 years remaining

Condition scale:

Range of years:

| 0 | 1 | | 4 | | | 8 | | | 12 |

Mid Point
Assumed Age   2.0   6   10

B. 5-TIERED SYSTEM 1—5

In the 5-tiered inspection system each component or system is given a grade, 1-5, and then the typical life of the component is looked up in the life charts and the midpoint of each of those equal time periods is assigned as the remaining economic life.

EXAMPLE

20%   12 year life

2 condition   8.4 years remaining

Condition scale:

Range of years:

| | 1 | | 2 | | 3 | | 4 | | 5 | |
| 0 | | 2.4 | | 4.8 | | 7.2 | | 9.6 | |

12

Mid Point   1.2   3.6   6.0   8.4   10.8
Assumed Age

ASSUMED AGE

TABLE LIFE	INSPECTION GRADE		
	THREE TIER MIDPOINTS		
	A	B	C
10	1.5	5	8
15	2.5	7.5	12.5
20	3.3	10	16.5
25	4.2	12.6	21
30	5	15	25
35	6	17.6	29
40	6.5	20	33
50	8	25	42

TABLE LIFE	INSPECTION GRADE				
	FIVE TIER MIDPOINT				
	1	2	3	4	5
10	1	3	5	7	9
15	1.5	4.5	7.5	10.5	13.5
20	2	6	10	14	18
25	2.5	7.5	12.5	17.5	22.5
30	3	9	15	21	27
35	3.5	10.5	17.5	24.5	31.5
40	4	12	20	28	36
50	5	15	25	35	45

C. ± TWO YEAR AGING—BEST ESTIMATE

If you have personnel or have hired consultants who have done a great number of inspections and can age systems or components or provide accurate estimates of the actual remaining life, you could then use the comparative appraisal method. This would involve inspecting the components, talking to the maintenance personnel, investigating preventative maintenance practices and sometimes site testing to verify the physical age of a component. This is then used as the age in the calculations.

EXAMPLE:
Field Evaluation ± 2 Year
    12 year life
    8 ± 2 years left per inspection

POLICY OPTION: FUTURE IMPROVEMENTS

Policy Question 7: How shall we incorporate, known and potential additional standards into our CNA?

1. No Considerations

2. Known Only (i.e. current code requirements)

3. Known, Projected and 12% Contingency

Advantages

_____
_____
_____

Concerns

_____
_____
_____

Recommendations

_____
_____
_____

TYPICAL FUTURE IMPROVEMENTS
TO CONSIDER IN CNAs

A 10% contingency is essential and up to 30% can be used to cover . . . .

Haz Mat Mitigation
– Asbestos—ceiling sprays, insulation, tile, roofing felts
– Lead Paint—interior and exterior paint

Building Code
– Electric requirements/GFCI/Arc fault
– Stair and railing improvements
– Backup generators

Life Safety
– Fire separation between units/floors/groupings
– Fire sprinklers & alarms—upgrades and communication
– Security lighting—stairs, halls, site
– Disaster reinforcement—hurricane, flood, wildfire, etc.

Healthy Homes
– 10 top low cost improvements
– Locking medicine cabinet
– Universal Design
– Fall prevention for all units

Energy Efficiency
– Upgrade central equipment
– Sub meter all utilities
– Model energy code requirements
– Reconfigure windows—eliminate
– Filtered ventilation air

Marketability
– Internet wireless
– Parking
– Public space—landscaping
– Lobby improvements
– Management office
– Upgraded appliances

POLICY OPTION: CAPITAL VS. MAINTENANCE

Policy Question 8: What repairs and replacements are to be funded with capital and which are maintenance items?

1. Use IRS definition

2. Select maintenance items from list

3. It is all maintenance until scheduled renovations

Advantages

_____
_____
_____

Concerns

_____
_____
_____

Recommendations

_____
_____
_____

CAPITAL NEEDS ASSESSMENT

WHAT TO CAPITALIZE AND WHAT'S MAINTENANCE? WORKSHEET

USING YOUR FIELD INSPECTION SHEET:

Maintenance or Capital Item

- Take 10-12 minutes, as an individual, for your project

- Using the CNA spreadsheet

- Identify any maintenance items *not* to be capitalized.

POLICY OPTIONS WORKSHEET

#1 What method shall we use to calculate our replacement reserve?

_____

#2 What rate of inflation shall we assume? _____

#3 What is our renovation style?

_____

_____

#4 How much deferred and unfunded maintenance, repairs and replacements will we allow?

_____

_____

#5 How will we grade and analyze the remaining economic life of our building parts?

_____

_____

#6 What is our required precision in evaluating remaining economic life?

_____

_____

#7 How shall we incorporate, known and projected future standards into our CNA?

_____

_____

#8 What is a capital replacement and what is maintenance?

_____

_____

FIELD INSPECTION PREPARATION

–   Logistics Set-Up

–   Policy Assumptions Sheet Completed for this Property?

Site personnel to meet us:
Energy maintenance supervisor
On-site manager

–   Goals: Collect sufficient data to:

1. Itemize quantity of components on this property
2. Rate condition of each component

–   Tools

3. Laser tape measure
4. Tapes, binoculars, clipboards
5. Digital camera
6. Blueprints (optional, but great when available)
7. AIA G—702—703 final draw from initial cost

–   Norms with Tenants

8. Respectful
9. No negative comments in field
10. Ask questions
11. Thank people

CASE STUDY CALCULATIONS
#2
QUICK & DIRTY OPTIONS

Replacement Cost

Initial Development Cost $ _____

Increase to Present Date ___ years x ___% cost   _____ % increase

        Add ___% for code, marketing   _____ % increase

Today's Replacement Cost $ ═══════════

Annual Reserve Calculations

Local Benchmark $ _____ PUPA
_____
_____

50-Year Sum of Digits $ _____ PUPA
_____
_____

Replacement Index $ _____ PUPA
_____
_____

LIFE, UNITS & COST

EXTERIOR CLOSURE

    Brick

        4.1-504-2020-Repoint Brick

        25 year CSF $741

    Wood Siding

        4.1-528-2010—Replace and paint clapboard

        25 year CSF $762

    Stucco—synthetic

        4.1-552-2020

        10 year CSF $367

    Recaulking

        41-572—opening—first floor

        20 year EA $10.23

        Second Floor

        20 year EA $93

    Metal Fire Escape

        4.4-140-2010—refinish flight

        7 year $357

    Fire Escape—stair and platform

        4.4-140-2020

        25 year Floor $5,485

    Wood Exterior Door—3'0 x 7'0

        4.6-420-1030

        40 year EA $1,053

WINDOWS

    Wood—rework

        4.7-230-1020

        15 year EA $197.50

    Wood—replace—2nd floor

        4.7-230-2040

        40 year EA $418

ROOFING

    BUR—Minor replacement 25%

        5.1-105-0500

        15 year SQ $568

Replacement
5.1-105-0700
28 year SQ $543
Elastomeric membrane repair 25%
5.1-235-0600
20 year SQ $653
Total replacement
5.1-235-0700
25 year SQ $493

EXTERIOR HARDWARE
Replace door closer
4.9-410-1010
15 year EA $235
Repair steel door
6.4-210-1010
14 year EA $164

INTERIOR CONSTRUCTION
Replace hollow core door
6.4-410-1030
30 year EA $297
Replace door hardware
6.4-720-0010
30 year EA $275
Repair vinyl wallpaper 2%
6.5-440-0010
8 year SF $234
Replace vinyl wallpaper
6.5-440-0020
15 year CSF $295
Repair acoustic tile—2%
6.7-310-0010
9 year CSF $484
Replace acoustic tile
6.7-310-0020
20 year CSF $304

Replace vinyl floor
      6.6-240-0020
      18 year SY $77
Regrout ceramic
      6.6-310-0010
      15 year CSF $685
Wood—refinish
      6.6-520-0020
      10 year SF $4.37

Replace carpet
      6.6-910-0020
      8 year SY $34.60
Replace kitchen cabinets and counter—up & down
      37 year LF $245

CONVEYING
Rebuild elevator—hydraulic
      25 year EA Floor $5,700
Rebuild elevator—electric
      25 year EA Floor $11,000

PLUMBING
Rework commode—tank type
      8.1-212-0030
      15 year EA $76
Replace commode—tank type
      8.1-212-0050
      35 year EA $365
Replace faucet—bath lavatory
      8.1-214-0040
      10 year EA $108
Replace shower valve
      8.1-220-0030
      10 year EA $260
Replace tub fiberglass
      8.1-229-0070
      20 year EA $1,151

Replace Circulation pump
    8.1-262-0030
    20 year EA $2,001
Replace water heater—gas, 30 gal
    8.1-283-0030
    10 year EA $841
Replace water heater—electric, 120 gal
    8.1-287-0030
    15 year EA $5,257
Replace sprinkler head
    8.1-851-1030
    20 year EA $59

HVAC SYSTEM

Repair boiler—gas, 250 MBH
    8.3-402-1010
    7 year EA $1,640
Replace boiler—gas, 250 MBH
    8.3-402-1010
    30 year EA $5,650
Repair furnace—gas, 100 MBH
    8.3-424-2010
    10 year EA $963

Replace furnace—gas, 100 MBH
    8.3-424-2030
    15 year EA $1,261
Replace wall furnace—electric
    9.8-721-0030
    20 EA $390
Replace vent fan—375 CFM
    8.5-311-1010
    15 year EA $439
Repair heat pump—1.5 ton
    8.6-170-1010
    10 year EA $1,617
Replace heat pump—1.5 ton
    8.6-170-1030
    20 year EA $3,500

ELECTRIC

Replace switch/outlet
9.5-710-0020/0010
20 year EA $45
Replace electric fixture
9.6-110-0030
20 year EA $102
Replace smoke detector
9.6-212-0030
15 year EA $186

PARKING LOT

Seal coat and repair
12.2-105-1010
5 year 10,000 SF $3,180
Repair and resurface
12.2-105-1010
10 year MSF $490
Replace Sidewalk
12.7-141-0100
25 year LF

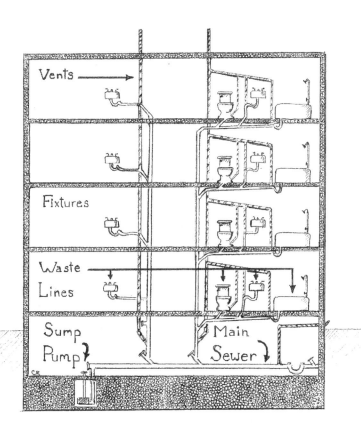

AS BUILTS

Building plans, especially the as-builts, are wonderful tools to accelerate take off quantities. Most of us can easily count the number of commodes and sinks. It is the hidden piping, controls, sump pumps, and back-up systems identified on the plans that are not always obvious to a field inspector. It is easy to miss the 273 valves on the water supply which isolates it from various units or the return loop on the hot water lines.

FIELD INSPECTION: THE MISSING SECTION

Take-off Estimates. Alas, I cannot accompany you and help count the squares of roofing or find the original building plans which are immensely helpful in taking off quantities. The first step is the same activity that contractors do called take-off estimating. If you are lucky enough to have the plans, you can fill in many of the quantities before you get to the site. From the plans, you can count the number of stoves, the number of windows, the number of doors, etc. You can measure the amount of hall space without needing a helper. It is most accurate if you have the final as-built plans.

Field Inspection. During the field inspection, I suggest at least a 2-person team. The first task to input component quantities in the spreadsheet column #8. If you don't have any of a specific component, insert a 0. The next step is to input the effective age in column Z per your policy criteria. Is it 3-year, 5-year or an actual estimate of the remaining economic life?

In all cases, you should be accompanied by the property superintendent and/or maintenance personnel. Since you'll only sample the units, you may see the best, but the site personnel knows the other 50% are seriously distressed.

Spreadsheet Template. The goal on the following spreadsheet template is to collect data for all the shaded green cells and don't touch the other cells. When you are finished, you will have a projection of the capital hard costs for the next 50 years.

As you are completing lots of fieldwork and massive data input, you don't always know where you are going. The goal is create a simple graphic. Ask Excel to chart the resulting expenses so you can visualize where your money is going. Then you can add your current reserves and your reserve payments over the time period and watch as they attempt to catch up with the ever-expanding capital demands of the structure.

URC: **Marvin - 2013 - 1.3**
Replacement Reserve Unit Cost Chart
2013

Building Components	Estimated Life (years)	Effective Age (years)	Estimated Remaining Life (years)	2013 Per Component Replacement Cost	Estimated Annual Increase	(At Term) Per Component Replacement Cost	Repl Factor (1, 3, Curve, HTL)	Number of Components	Total at Term Replacement Account	Annual Replacement Reserve	Monthly Replacement Reserve
Building Envelope											
Siding - Wood	40	15.00		$ 240.00 SQ	$ 7.20						
Siding - Vinyl	40	15.00		$ 3.40 SQ	$ 0.10						
Siding - Fiber Cement	50	15.00		$ 3.20 SQ	$ 0.10						
Recaulking/Repointing	20	2.00	18.00	$ 7.00 SF	$ 0.21	$ 10.78	1	27,000	$ 291,060.00	$ 16,170.00	$ 1,347.50
Doors- Replace Steel	40	20.00	20.00	$ 1,010.00 EA	$ 30.30	$ 1,616.00	1	17	$ 27,472.00	$ 1,373.60	$ 114.47
Door Hardware	15			$ 28.00 EA	$ 0.84						
Door- Storm	12			$ 295.00 EA	$ 8.85						
Window Replace - Vinyl	40	10.00	30.00	$ 328.00 EA	$ 9.84	$ 623.20	1	160	$ 99,712.00	$ 3,323.73	$ 276.98
Windows - Storm	15			$ 48.00 EA	$ 1.44						
Roof - Shingle - 30 Year	30	8.00	22.00	$ 208.00 SQ	$ 6.24	$ 345.28	1	30	$ 10,358.40	$ 470.84	$ 39.24
Roof Built Up	20			$ 250.00 SQ	$ 7.50						
Roof - Elastomeric EPDM	20	4.00	16.00	$ 220.00 SQ	$ 6.60	$ 325.60	1	910	$ 296,296.00	$ 18,518.50	$ 1,543.21
Chimney Repoint	30			$ 6.00 SF	$ 0.18						
Paint	10			$ 0.35 SF	$ 0.01						
Balconies/Deck/Escapes	40	20.00	20.00	$ 9.00 SF	$ 0.27	$ 14.40	1	2,000	$ 28,800.00	$ 1,440.00	$ 120.00
Gutter & Downspout	25	20.00	5.00	$ 3.85 LF	$ 0.12	$ 4.43	1	2,400	$ 10,626.00	$ 2,125.20	$ 177.10
Wood Trim	20			$ 3.70 LF	$ 0.11						
x				$ -	$ -						
x				$ -	$ -						
x				$ -	$ -						
x				$ -	$ -						
x				$ -	$ -						
x				$ -	$ -						
								Subtotal	$ 764,324.40	$ 43,421.87	$ 3,618.49

Building Site											
Sewer/Septic 1,000 sf Field	30		10.00	$ 5,200.00	EA	$ 156.00	$ 11.70	1	$ 196,595.10	$ 19,659.51	$ 1,638.29
Parking - Asphalt	25	15.00	3.00	$ 9.00	SY	$ 0.27	$ 3.05	1	$ 48,832.00	$ 16,277.33	$ 1,356.44
Parking Seal Coat	10	7.00	24.00	$ 2.80	SY	$ 0.08	$ 8.43	1	$ 10,956.40	$ 456.52	$ 38.04
Sidewalks	40	16.00	12.00	$ 4.90	SF	$ 0.15					
Exterior Lighting Pole	20	8.00	6.00	$ 400.00	EA	$ 12.00	$ 544.00	1	$ 7,616.00	$ 634.67	$ 52.89
Play Equipment	12	6.00		$ 18,000.00	EA	$ 540.00	$ 21,240.00	1	$ 21,240.00	$ 3,540.00	$ 295.00
Fencing Board	16		14.00	$ 18.00	LF	$ 0.54					
Slabs Concrete/Steps	30	16.00		$ 6.20	SF	$ 0.19	$ 8.80	1	$ 18,488.40	$ 1,320.60	$ 110.05
Sports Equipment	15		19.00			$ -					
Mailboxes	20	1.00		$ 83.00	EA	$ 2.49	$ 130.31	1	$ 6,515.50	$ 342.92	$ 28.58
Well Pump/Equipment	15			$ 2,100.00	EA	$ 63.00					
Curb Cut	30		1.00	$ 750.00	EA	$ 22.50					
Signage	15	14.00		$ 8,660.00	EA	$ 259.80	$ 8,919.80	1	$ 8,919.80	$ 8,919.80	$ 743.32
x				$ -		$ -	$ -				
x				$ -		$ -	$ -				
x				$ -		$ -	$ -				
x				$ -		$ -	$ -				
							Subtotal	$ 319,163.20	$ 51,151.35	$ 4,262.61	

Common Area											
Laminate Flooring	18	1.00	17.00	$ 4.80	SF	$ 0.14	$ 7.25	1	$ 86,976.00	$ 5,116.24	$ 426.35
Carpet - Replace	8		5.00	$ 19.00	SY	$ 0.57					
Paint	7	2.00	13.00	$ 0.30	SF	$ 0.01	$ 0.35	1	$ 5,865.00	$ 1,173.00	$ 97.75
Electrical Fixtures	25	12.00		$ 22.00	EA	$ 0.66	$ 30.58	1	$ 6,116.00	$ 470.46	$ 39.21
Laundry Equipment	12			$ 540.00	EA	$ 16.20					
Water Heater 40 gal	15			$ 485.00	EA	$ 14.55					
Sprinkler Heads ea	18	1.00	17.00	$ 80.00	EA	$ 2.40	$ 120.80	1	$ 84,560.00	$ 4,974.12	$ 414.51
Security System 3 Zone	15	1.00	14.00	$ 9,400.00	EA	$ 282.00	$ 13,348.00	1	$ 133,480.00	$ 9,534.29	$ 794.52
Mailboxes	35			$ 1,000.00	EA	$ 30.00					
Bathroom Fixtures	16			$ 600.00	Allow	$ 18.00					
Furnishings	14	4.00	10.00	$ 50,000.00	Allow	$ 1,500.00	$ 65,000.00	1	$ 65,000.00	$ 6,500.00	$ 541.67
Lawn Sprinkler	20			$ 0.90	SF	$ 0.03					
Stairway - Paint	27	16.00	11.00	$ 2,400.00	Allow	$ 72.00	$ 3,192.00	1	$ 19,152.00	$ 1,741.09	$ 145.09
Stairway - Carpet Landings				$ 19.00	SF	$ 0.57					
Stairway - Carpet Steps				$ 1.50	EA	$ 0.05					
Community Area	10	5.00	5.00	$ 30,000.00	Allow	$ 900.00	$ 34,500.00	1	$ 34,500.00	$ 6,900.00	$ 575.00
x				$ -		$ -	$ -				
x				$ -		$ -	$ -				
x				$ -		$ -	$ -				
x				$ -		$ -	$ -				
								$ 435,649.00	$ 36,409.19	$ 3,034.10	

Common Mechanical/Electrical											
Forced Air Gas	25		$ 4.00	SF	$ 0.12						
Pump 1HSP	15	20.00	$ 4,000.00	EA	$ 120.00						
Boiler System 680K	30	10.00	$ 36,400.00	EA	$ 1,092.00	$ 47,320.00	1	2	$ 94,640.00	$ 9,464.00	$ 788.67
Cooling System 3 Ton	15		$ 9,000.00	EA	$ 270.00						
Cooling System 1 Ton	20	10.00	$ 3,000.00	EA	$ 90.00	$ 3,900.00	1				
Central Water Heat 100 GPH	10	9.00	$ 5,000.00	EA	$ 150.00	$ 6,350.00	1	2	$ 12,700.00	$ 1,411.11	$ 117.59
Electric Service 400 Amp	50		$ 8,000.00	EA	$ 240.00						
Emergency Lighting W/ Battery	25		$ 250.00	EA	$ 7.50						
Plumbing Waste/Supply	50		$ 645.00		$ 19.35						
Sprinkler System	40	20.00	$ 6.00	SF	$ 0.18	$ 9.60	1	30,000	$ 288,000.00	$ 14,400.00	$ 1,200.00
Elevator 2500 lbs	50		$ 25,000.00	/Flr	$ 750.00						
A/C Installation	40		$ 4,000.00	EA	$ 120.00						
Electrical 800 Amp	40	28.00	$ 23,000.00	EA	$ 690.00	$ 42,320.00	1	1	$ 42,320.00	$ 1,511.43	$ 125.95
Electrical 200 Amp	40	12.00	$ 5,100.00	EA	$ 153.00						
Electrical 100 Amp	40	30.00	$ 860.00	EA	$ 25.80	$ 1,634.00	1	60	$ 98,040.00	$ 3,268.00	$ 272.33
x			$ -		$ -						
x			$ -		$ -						
x			$ -		$ -						
x			$ -		$ -						
x			$ -		$ -						
x			$ -		$ -						
Subtotal									$ 652,700.00	$ 41,754.54	$ 3,479.54

Unit Interior												
Exhaust Fan	12.5	1.00	11.50	EA	$ 114.00	$ 3.42	$ 153.33	1	54	$ 8,279.82	$ 719.98	$ 60.00
Commodes - Replace	35	20.00	15.00	EA	$ 350.00	$ 10.50	$ 507.50	1	106	$ 53,795.00	$ 3,586.33	$ 298.86
Medicine Cabinet	20	5.00	15.00	EA	$ 87.00	$ 2.61	$ 126.15	1	54	$ 6,812.10	$ 454.14	$ 37.85
Miscellaneous					$ -	$ -						
Unit Flooring - Vinyl	18	1.00	7.00	SF	$ 3.60	$ 0.11	$ 16.94	1	1,110	$ 18,803.40	$ 2,686.20	$ 223.85
Unit Flooring - Carpet	8			SY	$ 14.00	$ 0.42						
Unit Flooring - Wood Refinish	20	10.00	20.00	SF	$ 3.00	$ 0.09	$ 46.40	1	200	$ 9,280.00	$ 464.00	$ 38.67
Electrical Fixtures Allow.	30			EA	$ 29.00	$ 0.87						
Outlets/Switches	30	1.00	14.00	EA	$ 12.00	$ 0.36						
Smoke Detector	15			EA	$ 66.00	$ 1.98	$ 93.72	1	100	$ 9,372.00	$ 669.43	$ 55.79
Service Panel 125 Amp	50			EA	$ 725.00	$ 21.75						
Electrical Heat - Baseboard	20	12.00	8.00	EA	$ 168.00	$ 5.04	$ 694.40	1	41	$ 28,470.40	$ 3,558.80	$ 296.57
HVAC - AC Units	20	10.00	20.00	EA	$ 560.00	$ 16.80	$ 864.00	1	60	$ 51,840.00	$ 2,592.00	$ 216.00
Entrance Doors	30	10.00	20.00	EA	$ 540.00	$ 16.20	$ 336.00	1	150	$ 50,400.00	$ 2,520.00	$ 210.00
Unit Doors	30	10.00	20.00	EA	$ 210.00	$ 6.30	$ 44.80	1	150	$ 6,720.00	$ 336.00	$ 28.00
Unit Hardware	30			EA	$ 28.00	$ 0.84						
Blinds	8			EA	$ 52.00	$ 1.56						
CC Kitchens & Restrooms	30	3.00	27.00		$ 72,000.00	$ 2,160.00	$ 130,320.00	1	1	$ 130,320.00	$ 4,826.67	$ 402.22
CC Furnishings	20	3.00	17.00		$ 35,000.00	$ 1,050.00	$ 52,850.00	1	1	$ 52,850.00	$ 3,108.82	$ 259.07
CC Office & Equipment	5	3.00	2.00		$ 34,000.00	$ 1,020.00	$ 36,040.00	1	1	$ 36,040.00	$ 18,020.00	$ 1,501.67
CC Mechanical Systems	25	5.00	20.00		$ 35,000.00	$ 1,050.00	$ 56,000.00	1	1	$ 56,000.00	$ 2,800.00	$ 233.33
x					$ -	$ -						
x					$ -							
x												
									Subtotal	$ 518,982.72	$ 46,342.38	$ 3,861.86

Unit Interior												
Kitchen - Stove 30"	18	1.00	17.00	$ 340.00	EA	$ 10.20	513.40	50	1	$ 25,670.00	$ 1,510.00	$ 125.83
Kitchen - Refrigerator 16 CF	14	1.00	13.00	$ 550.00	EA	$ 16.50	764.50	50	1	$ 38,225.00	$ 2,940.38	$ 245.03
Kitchen - Dishwasher	10	1.00	9.00	$ 395.00	EA	$ 11.85	501.65	50	1	$ 25,082.50	$ 2,786.94	$ 232.25
Kitchen - Garbage Disposal	10	1.00	9.00	$ 165.00	EA	$ 4.95	209.55	50	1	$ 10,477.50	$ 1,164.17	$ 97.01
Kitchen - Faucet	10	1.00	9.00	$ 103.00	EA	$ 3.09	130.81	50	1	$ 6,540.50	$ 726.72	$ 60.56
Kitchen - Vent Hood	15	5.00	10.00	$ 146.00	EA	$ 4.38	189.80	50	1	$ 9,490.00	$ 949.00	$ 79.08
Kitchen -				$ -		$ -						
Kitchen Cabinets	24	1.00	23.00	$ 147.00	LF	$ 4.41	248.43	1,200	1	$ 298,116.00	$ 12,961.57	$ 1,080.13
Kitchen - Countertop	24	1.00	23.00	$ 24.00	LF	$ 0.72	40.56	600	1	$ 24,336.00	$ 1,058.09	$ 88.17
Kitchen - Floor	12	1.00	11.00	$ 3.60	SF	$ 0.11	4.79	4,000	1	$ 19,152.00	$ 1,741.09	$ 145.09
Bathroom Flooring	18	1.00	17.00	$ 3.60	SF	$ 0.11	5.44	2,000	1	$ 10,872.00	$ 639.53	$ 53.29
Tub & Surrounds	20	5.00	15.00	$ 985.00	EA	$ 29.55	1,428.25	54	1	$ 77,125.50	$ 5,141.70	$ 428.48
Vanity	22	5.00	17.00	$ 450.00	EA	$ 13.50	679.50	54	1	$ 36,693.00	$ 2,158.41	$ 179.87
Diverter Valve/Drain	10	1.00	9.00	$ 210.00	EA	$ 6.30	266.70	54	1	$ 14,401.80	$ 1,600.20	$ 133.35
Vanity Faucet	10	1.00	9.00	$ 86.00	EA	$ 2.58	109.22	54	1	$ 5,897.88	$ 655.32	$ 54.61
Water Heater - Electrical 40 gal	15			$ 485.00	EA	$ 14.55						
x				$ -		$ -						
x				$ -		$ -						
x				$ -		$ -						
x				$ -		$ -						
x				$ -		$ -						
									Subtotal	$ 602,079.68	$ 36,033.12	$ 3,002.76
Improvements by 2020												
Décor	15	6.50	8.50	$111,660.00	EA	$ 3,349.80	140,133.30	1	1	$ 140,133.30	$ 16,486.27	$ 1,373.86
Elevator #2	20	1.00	19.00	$165,000.00	EA	$ 4,950.00	259,050.00	1	1	$ 259,050.00	$ 13,634.21	$ 1,136.18
Energy Star	40	25.00	15.00	$100,000.00	LS	$ 3,000.00	145,000.00	1	1	$ 145,000.00	$ 9,666.67	$ 805.56
									Subtotal	$ 544,183.30	$ 39,787.15	$ 3,315.60
									TOTAL	$ 3,837,082.30	$ 294,899.59	$ 24,574.97

Chapter 7

ASSET MANAGEMENT HANDBOOK

SPREADSHEET ANALYSIS

Theme:	The truth is in the numbers and the graph they draw.
Learning Objectives:	• How to analyze replacement data to prepare for: — Annual capital plans — Refinancing — Sale/merger
Essential Vocabulary:	— Refinance — Deferred Repairs — Proactive Maintenance

SPREADSHEET MESSAGES

Not Fantasy. And while it may be useful to politicians to develop propaganda to cover up the inevitable expenditures in government operations, that just guarantees your bankruptcy. Stephen Covey's first habit was "Be proactive." Either you save the money to fix the roof when it begins to leak or you have a source to borrow the money based on your very positive cash flow or you don't. If no funds are available, the building begins its quickening spiral into disuse, abandonment and eventual destruction. Property ownership and asset management, like life, are an ongoing game of: balancing, juggling, standing in the 3-ring circus, always trying to maintain critical feasibility standards. All buildings, like all corporations, eventually fail along an established path. It is not difficult to track and plot the stage of life of your buildings.

Basic Guidelines. While I very strongly advocate that we use accurate field measurements of the reserve needs of your structures, there are some basic rules of thumb that you should not ignore. In family housing, almost all structures need major internal renovation between Year 14 and 18. In all structures, a substantial full refurbishment of all systems is required between Year 32 and 38. If you are not planning for significant improvements during these time periods, you are planning to fail and to experience significant management and asset management pain during the process.

Underwriting. If you can hang on and extend the pain for a significant time, you might earn the reputation of the worst slum landlord in town. As you begin to: cannibalize units, raise fees and promote rapid evictions while allowing the heat to go off in the hallways, the elevators to break down for weeks, stiff the tax man, and whenever you can, the water bills your reputation will grow.

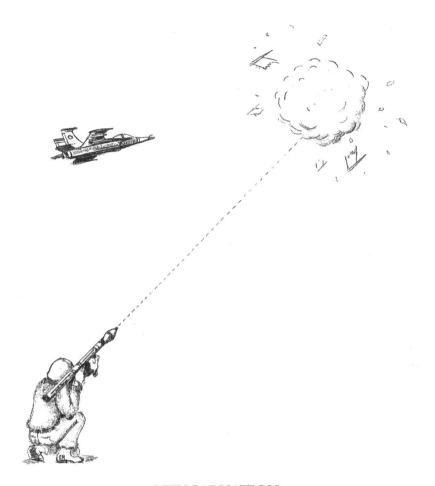

REINCARNATION

The Replacement Reserve spreadsheet always projects the same phenomenon. The rents, the reserves, and the owner's savings reach a point where they can no longer pay for the rapidly depreciating structure. This illustration suggests destruction. It is really the beginning of a new property with the massive improvements that are required within the old shell. Nonprofits have already owned portfolios where they have added elevators, central air conditioning, internet connections, cable TV, security, parking, dishwashers or refrigerators, none of which were provided in the initially constructed 1914 3-story walk up. To be reincarnated, one must be replaced. It is inevitable, so plan on it and you will guide your organization through many lives.

Example Spreadsheet Graph Analysis
Harmony Place

Our Example. Here we have a 50-year capital needs spreadsheet in graphic form that has been prepared with a 3% inflation assumption and no contingency for improvements in design or life safety over that time period. What do we see? Learn and divine.

First Wave—Year 2. The very first is that in 2005, approximately Year 2, they have $245,000 of deferred maintenance coming due. If they are going to finance this need, it is essential to pick up the $50,000 due in 2006 and 2007. So add another $100,000 to the base. Now as we review need in years 2010, 11, 12, 13 we suggest packaging a preservation loan source of $245,000 plus $100,000 plus another $70,000 or a total of $415,000 of rehab hard costs. The soft costs of both acquiring the loan and overseeing the work are estimated to be about 35%. So multiply the $415K by 1.35%. Now we are starting out with a $560,000 loan package that we should be working on immediately. We've just quantified the first refinance.

The Second Refinance. There are 3 relatively large peaks coming up. You can see one in 2015, a double peak in 2019 and 2020, and a significant peak in 2027.

We could look at the spreadsheet to identify the components that require replacement during that time period. We must do that to develop a scope of work. As far as financial forecasting, it looks like in approximately 2020, 15 years after our first refinance, we should put all of the identified needs, (everything listed from 2013 to 2030) into a loan package that we set up to close probably in 2021. It looks like it is going to have $950,000 in hard costs. Using our 1.35% soft cost rule of thumb, (sometimes dangerous, so make your own) on this property we'll need about $1,300,000 for its second go-around which we are projecting in 2021.

The Last Pass in our Projection. Unfortunately, some 30-year items are going to come due in 2034 but we start having significant need in 2032. If we're going to try and handle this property, in 2035 is going to be the requirement for a substantial gut rehab/replacement of all major items. We should even be looking way beyond that. This time, we're taking

2035 and we're going to pick up all of the replacement needs from 2032 through 2042. We're going to knock it all off with one huge renovation. You can figure we are now at 2030, 33, 34, 35, 36?? So maybe $750K in hard cost, but at this point, a lot has gone on in the world. It is very likely there are going to be 30% more code requirements and market amenities. In this case, to our $750K add an additional 30% and we're up to $975K. Our soft costs are on top of that. So we're projecting in the year 2035 another $1.3 million hard cost and soft cost job without relocation.

Relocation Temporary Cost? If replacement of these items requires relocation, it is quite easily going to cost 50% more to complete this job with the tenants in place assuming Uniform Relocation Act protections and multiple staging by the subcontractors. That pops it right up to the $2 million range. That is what we should consider borrowing and planning for pass 3.

The other alternative is leave it to the next guy.

Scope of Work

So what components are creating the $240,000 need in the Year 2005? We can look back on our spreadsheets for the very large numbers in the column for that year. In Year 1, we have roofing, a little bit of vinyl flooring, a significant amount of kitchen improvements and some replacement of the exterior building front doors. With just the roofs, kitchens, baths, this 18-unit building requires $241,000 in immediate repairs. Looking back to our rules of thumb suggesting that to this we must add a 10% contingency and 30% soft costs gets us in the $560,000 range or $28,800 per unit—a pretty significant number in 2004.

Risk Mitigation—3 Steps

Identify it. In this case it is the wearing out of building components and equipment faster than we can afford to replace them.

Quantify the risk. Things seem bigger and scarier if they are unknown. We know right now that we need $28,000 per unit, and if we do, we can have a healthy property for another 10 years. It is not the end of the world. It might be difficult. It might seem like there are very few options, but at least we know the constraints and the goals.

Defeat the risk. That means we might be negotiating options with our lenders. We might be asking some notes to be forgiven or subordinated to allow new money to flow. We may be considering extensive fundraising. One way or the other, be it volunteers or a resyndication, our primary objective is to defeat this risk or this job is over.

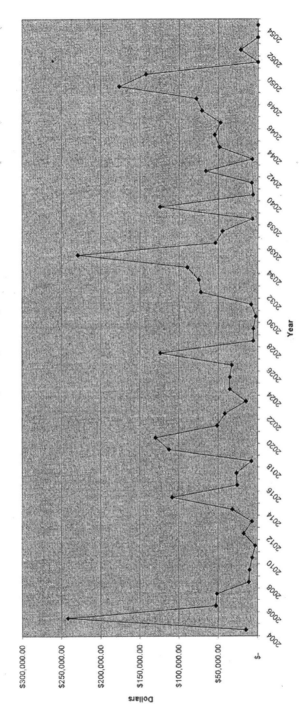

HARMONY PLACE
Capital Needs Assessment
Total Anticipated Expenses by Year

Chapter 8

ASSET MANAGEMENT HANDBOOK

RISK RANKING

Theme: A quick overview makes for a productive analysis.

Learning Objectives: • To Chart Our Current Status

                            • To Introduce Portfolio-Wide Template

Essential Vocabulary: — Performing
                            — Expense Coverage Ratio
                            — Working Capital
                            — Guarantee Requirements

Exhibit 6-4: Early Warning Signs to Identify Failing Property Performance

Performance Indicator	Performance Standard (typical)	Early Warning Signs
Tenant receivables	Owners should collect 95 percent of the property's gross potential rent.	Tenant receivables above this level suggest that the property is not receiving all available income, and may quickly make it difficult for property managers to pay bills on time, or make required reserves deposits. *Possible causes:* Lax management/rent collection efforts; or tenants' inability to pay due to unemployment/ problems in the local economy.
Unit turnaround	Vacant units should be re-rented in three to fourteen days.	Slow unit turnaround results in a loss of income for the property. *Possible causes:* Management issues (such as poor communication between maintenance and office management) or marketing difficulties (e.g., finding qualified tenants).
Vacancy rate	Properties should be 95 percent occupied, as indicated on occupancy reports and rent rolls.	Higher vacancy rates result in a loss of income for the property. *Possible causes:* Management problems, marketing issues, neighborhood decline.
Accounts payable	Majority of accounts are paid in a timely manner; 30-day or more delinquent accounts are pursued by management promptly.	Increasing or high accounts payable and numerous past due accounts because the property is not paying its bills on time. *Possible causes:* Property manager is not collecting all available sources of revenue, or rents do not adequately cover the property's expenses.
Capital needs expenditures	Capital needs are addressed in a timely manner and based on a capital needs assessment / useful life analysis and schedule.	Increasing or unexpected capital needs, or capital needs that are out of line with the budget and/or the planned timing of capital improvements. *Possible causes:* Poor initial planning; routine maintenance is not being performed. Note, the former will impact cash flow; the latter will result in premature systems and equipment failures.
Cash balance	Cash balance should be sufficient to cover anticipated monthly operating expenses.	Decreasing or low cash balances mean that a property will have difficulty covering expenses in the near future. *Possible causes:* Either decreasing income to the property or increasing expenses. The cause(s) should be evident from the property's monthly financial statement.
Property condition	Property should receive routine maintenance and remain in standard condition.	Deteriorating property condition or increase in code violations. *Possible causes:* Property does not have enough cash reserves to pay for needed maintenance or repairs, or poor management (i.e., the property manager is not addressing the property's maintenance needs). Poor physical condition of the property may result in violations of relevant local codes, which in turn violates HOME property standards requirements and may cause health and safety concerns for tenants. Ongoing neglect of the property's physical maintenance will lead to difficulties marketing the property to tenants.
Local economy and crime		Decline in the local economy that results in higher numbers of unemployed tenants and impacts rent collection; or increase in neighborhood crime that impacts the property's ability to attract good tenants, and also leads to problems collecting sufficient rent to cover expenses. Note, while the decline of the neighborhood can contribute to the decline if the property, so too can the decline of the property contribute to the stress or decline of a neighborhood.
Property management staff turnover		High or frequent staff turnover. *Possible causes:* Difficulties with managing the property.

INSPECTION INPUT

Risk Ranking Scale for Asset Managers

1. Outstanding

2. Strong

3. Performing

4. Marginal

5. Salvageable

6. Probable Loss

PORTFOLIO STATUS
OVERALL RISK RANKING AS OF *OCTOBER 2012*

Project	Rank	Priority	Issue 1	Issue 2	Solutions
12 Hopkins Street	Strong	3	Reserves inadequate	None	Increase replacement reserve funding
Green Court	Performing	2	High turnover	Cash flow reduction but still break even	Investigate addition amenities; offer year-end bonus
Cherry Avenue	Marginal	1	High economic vacancy, therefore, negative cash flow	Needs parking, other amenities to compete	Start negotiation with mortgage holder re: reapplication of payment to security

EXAMPLE
DETAILED RISK RANKING REPORT

RISK RANK 4.5	ADDRESS: 1703-B Front Street				CURRENT STATUS
	2009	2010	2011	2012	
Vacancy	5	4	4	5	18% vacancy
Collection Loss	5	4	4	5	21% loss
Cash Flow	4	3	4	5	Negative $6,000
Reserves	4	4	5	5	Not funded
Debt Coverage Ratio	5	5	5	5	Below 1.0
Sponsor Capacity	3	2	2	3	Showing strain
Asset Management	3	3	2	2	Just starting
Property Management	2	2	2	2	No major
Reporting	3	3	3	2	Late but accurate
Physical Condition	3	3	3	4	Showing age
Benchmarks	3	3	4	5	50%

Outstanding (1); Strong (2); Performing (3); Marginal (4); Salvageable (5); Probable Loss (6)

By: _____ Date: ____January 2012____

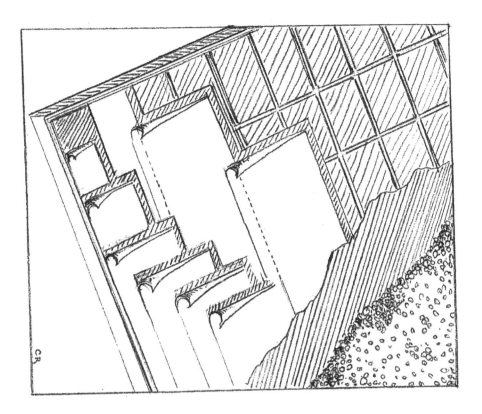

RISK OVERHEAD

What types of risk are involved when you push the replacement cycle so long that your built up roof begins to leak? Watch it for awhile. Maybe you can do partial replacement. Sooner or later that could cause secondary damage through the roof. Small leaks over long periods can rot wood, saturate insulation, fester stachybotrys mold, and other unwelcome creatures. Risk analysis is all about identifying what might happen, how serious could the damage be, and what, if anything, you can do about it.

OPERATIONS RISK RATING GUIDE

OUTSTANDING (1)

Description: This project is very strong and stable, is in no way impaired, and the likelihood of realizing all projected tax and ownership benefits is excellent.

Characteristics	Financial: Vacancies less than 5% of gross potential rent collection loss is less than 3% of effective gross rents. Cash flow funds all reserves and amortizing debt service with DCR of 1.25, plus some or all of the partnership management fee.
	Management: The owner demonstrates: 1) strong asset management; 2) proven management capacity, and 3) strong management succession. Property management is capable and efficient. The project owner is responsive, financially secure and is able to comfortably meet all guarantee requirements and contingent liabilities.
	Reporting: Limited partner reporting requirements are met on a timely basis with accurate reports.
	Physical: No compliance issues exist. The property is in excellent physical condition.
	Benchmarks: 95% of all benchmarks achieved many by 10% or more.
Asset Management Intervention	Review and analysis of quarterly reports. Annual random compliance review and site inspection. Written monitoring report annually based on year-end audit, site visit.

OPERATIONS RISK RATING GUIDE

STRONG (2)

Description: This project has minimal current problems or indications of deteriorating operational or financial conditions. It is performing as expected, and there is a good possibility of realizing all projected tax and ownership benefits.

Characteristics	Financial: Vacancies are no more than 7.5% of gross potential rent and collection loss is no more than 5%. Cash flow sufficient to cover amortizing debt and required reserve payments, with a DCR of at least 1.10.
	Management: Both the project and the owner have sufficient working capital and reserves to weather occasional market disturbances or other downturns. The sponsor is able to meet all guarantee requirements and contingent liabilities and the organization has sufficient capacity and depth. Asset management and/or property management is adequate to oversee the project.
	Reporting: Reports may occasionally be up to 15 days late, but are accurate.
	Physical: While there may be occasional signs of deferred maintenance or compliance issues, the sponsor addresses them promptly.
	Benchmarks: 80% of all benchmarks achieved.
Asset Management Intervention	Review and analysis of quarterly report.
	Annual random compliance review and site inspection.
	Written monitoring report annually based on year-end audit, site visit.

OPERATIONS RISK RATING GUIDE

PERFORMING (3)

Description: This project is just performing compared to initial projections and standard real estate performance standards. It will experience occasional weaknesses during the analysis period that should be monitored, but on the whole, presents little risk of financial loss.

Characteristics	Financial: Vacancy loss is 10% and collection loss is 7.5%. The project is just generating sufficient cash flow to break even, with a DCR of 1.0-1.1. Required reserves are underfunded, but the reserve balance is sufficient to cover occasional cash needs. Management: The owner's financial resources are modest, but it is able to cover its obligations. There may not be management depth, but the staff in place is capable. Asset management and property management require improvement in some areas, but are generally sufficient. Reporting: Reports are habitually 30-60 days late, but are mostly accurate. Physical: The physical condition of the property may have multiple deficiencies but the owner has developed a plan and identified sources of funds to address them. Minor, correctable compliance issues may be discovered. Benchmarking: Property is below standards in 5 to 7 areas.
Asset Management Intervention	Review and analysis of quarterly report. Annual random compliance review and site inspection. Written monitoring report annually based on year-end audit, site visit plus quarterly updates in database on risks identified.

OPERATIONS RISK RATING GUIDE

MARGINAL (4)

Description: This project exhibits signs of significant deterioration in operating and financial condition. It may continually underperform and require constant oversight and support. There is no *imminent* risk of financial loss.

Characteristics	
	Financial: Vacancy loss is 12%, collection loss is 10% and turnover may be frequent. Cash flow is at times insufficient to cover debt service (DCR of 1.0-0.90), resulting in occasional slippage (30 days or less) in debt payments. Required reserves are underfunded and unanticipated draws are being made. Accounts payable 10% or more of Effective Gross Income or general partner advances funds to cover occasional deficits.
	Management: The owner's financial condition may be weak or slipping. Both asset management and property management capacity requires improvement. Owner's coverage of guarantee requirements and contingent liabilities may be difficult.
	Reporting: 1-2 quarterly reports missing, or reports are habitually 30+ days late, and/or require corrections, explanations. The owner may also be somewhat unresponsive to partnership requests or requirements.
	Physical: The property has notable deficiencies that are not being addressed. Serious compliance issues may be discovered, units may be off-line 30-60 days and/or 8823's may have been issued, but the issues are correctable.
	Benchmarks that automatically qualify a project for this rating include: issuance of an 8823, unauthorized debt, unpaid real estate taxes (1-3 months), expired property insurance, notification of IRS audit or litigation involving the project limited partnership.

Asset Management Intervention	Review and analysis of quarterly report.
	Monthly review of operating statement.
	Biannual random compliance review and site inspection.
	Technical assistance to create action plan to health.

OPERATIONS RISK RATING GUIDE

SALVAGEABLE (5)

Description: This project exhibits signs of serious problems and requires a high level of monitoring and intervention. Loss of the project and/or tax credits is likely barring specific actions to strengthen the asset or the ownership entity such as a restructure or recapitalization (including significant financial assistance from the partnership and other funders.

Characteristics	Financial: Vacancy: 15%-20%; Collection loss: 12%-20%. Cash flow is insufficient to cover debt service. Reserves not funded or depleted. Accounts payable in excess of 20% of Estimated Gross Income. Mortgage payments may have slipped 30-60 days past due. Lenders may have issued default notices but are still willing to negotiate restructure terms.
	Management: Lack of effective asset management and/or property management impacting project-level operations and warrant change in managing agent. The owner's financial condition poor and coverage of guarantee requirements and contingent liabilities is unlikely. Management deficiencies may exist and removal may be warranted.
	Reporting: 1-2 quarterly reports missing, or reports are habitually 30+ days late, and/or require corrections, explanations. Several financial reports may be missing or serious misrepresentations discovered.
	Physical: The property's physical condition is poor. Serious compliance issues exist. 8823's may have been issued and units may have been offline 60 days or more.
	Benchmarks that automatically qualify a project for this rating include: issuance of an 8823 that may prove difficult or costly to cure, unpaid real estate taxes (over 6 months), expired property insurance (over 3 months), IRS audit that may result in a significant reduction in credits or recapture, serious litigation or other events that threaten to jeopardize the viability of the partnership.

Asset Management Intervention	• Review and analysis of monthly reporting. • Contact with lenders and funders. • In-depth reviews/visits to implement workout plan. • Replacement of management/partnership members. • Written monitoring report monthly. Senior management, workout staff, legal department and investment management appraised of significant problems by memo.

OPERATIONS RISK RATING GUIDE

PROBABLE LOSS (6)

Description: There is a high probability that the project will be lost through foreclosure or other action, and/or a significant amount of tax credits will be lost or recaptured.

Characteristics	<u>Financial</u>: All of Level 5 characteristics plus lenders may have initiated foreclosure actions or the project may be facing sheriff's sale for failure to pay real estate taxes. <u>Management</u>: The owner's organization may be on the brink of bankruptcy or dissolution, which will have a serious negative impact on the partnership's interest. <u>Reporting</u>: 1-2 quarterly reports missing, or reports are habitually 30+ days late, and/or require corrections, explanations. <u>Physical</u>: The project's physical condition may be extremely poor. The building may be considered unsafe, with severe code violations issued and units offline for 90 days or more. Severe and/or uncorrectable compliance issues exist. Recapture is highly likely. <u>Benchmarks</u>: 50 to 80% failure across the board.
Asset Management Intervention	• Review of monthly operating reports. • Quarterly compliance review and site inspection; more frequent or in-depth reviews/visits may be warranted. • Written monitoring report monthly. Senior management, workout staff, legal department and investment management kept appraised of significant developments directly by memo. • Refer to workout department; negotiation with lenders and funders.

Chapter 9

ASSET MANAGEMENT HANDBOOK

PRESERVATION SOLUTIONS

Theme:	Everything must be rejuvenated.
Learning Objectives:	• Identify 10 ways to rejuvenate property
	• Evaluate best options for your programs
Essential Vocabulary:	— Flexibility — Win-Win Negotiation
Assumed Experience:	Six months in real estate, property management, banking or development industry or two years of higher education

STRATEGIC PLANNNING

Revenues. Now that you have established when that next $4 million of improvements shall be required, you have to forecast how to pay for it. As you work with these spreadsheets you will realize that it is not possible to fund a replacement reserve to pay for the future renovation with low income rents. You can work the front end of the curve and put off the inevitable refinance for awhile. What replacement funds can you invest monthly? How much will you be able to borrow in the future?

At the same time, you must analyze the building use options at Year 40. In many of the properties that were developed 40 years ago, the highest and best use is to demolish the structure and build another 23 stories on top of the now highly urbanized plot of land.

20 Year Horizon. Organizations that think strategically decades into the future and have a clear crystal ball viewpoint, have gained significant financial independence due to the massive appreciation of their properties. Others, not so fortunate, have seen the same low value properties slowly bleed their financial coffers dry as they attempt to maintain the property, their goodwill with their lenders and their reputation in the community way beyond the time at which they must refinance and move on.

It's Just Math. It is not rocket science. It is very predictable. It is straight math. It is inevitable. The only unfortunate part is that institutional underwriters in both profit and nonprofit arenas have not fully understood the long-term effects of chintzy underwriting. Suicidal underwriting doesn't provide 20-year anxiety-free property operations. The unfortunate non-profit owners are left holding the bag with a tenant group who must live in rapidly decreasing quality units.

ASSET MANAGEMENT FOR SURVIVAL

THREE WAYS TO UNDERWRITE
CAPITAL SUBSIDY REQUIRED FOR SUSTAINABLE
DEVELOPMENT

80-UNIT PROPERTY
1/2013

	Historical Non-syndicated Total / Per Unit	Semi-Sustainable Tax Credits Total / Per Unit	20-Year Sustainable Life Total / Per Unit
Gross Potential Rent	$576,000 / $600/mo	$552,000 / $575/mo	$523,2000 / $545/mo
Rent Loss	($28,800) / 5%	($38,600) / 7%	($36,620) / 7%
Other Income	$8,000 / $100/yr	$8,000 / $100/yr	$2,000 / $25/yr
Effective Gross Income	$555,200	$521,400	$488,580
Operating Expenses	($220,000) / $2,750	($240,000) / $3,000	($336,000) / $4,200
Reserve Deposit	($20,000) / $250	($28,000) / $350	($40,800) / $510
Asset Management	0 / $0	($16,000) / $200	($20,000) / $250
Net Operating Income	$315,200	$237,400	$91,780
Debt Coverage Ratio	1.10	1.20	1.15
Debt Service	($286,500)	($197,800)	($78,013)
Operating Cash Flow	$28,700	$39,600	$13,760
% of Effective Gross Income	5.2%	7.6%	3.5%
Total Development Cost	$5,6000,000 / $70,000	$5,600,000 / $70,000	$5,600,000 / $70,000
Supportable Debt	($3,434,000)	($2,246,000)	($1,210,920)
Supportable Equity	0	($396,000)	($396,000)
Capital Subsidy Needed **% of Total Development Cost**	**$2,166,000 /** **$27,075** **39%**	**$2,958,000 /** **$36,975** **53%**	**$4,389,570 /** **$54,870** **77%**
Mortgage Interest Rate	6.00%	5.00%	5.00%
Loan Term	40	30	30
Credit Enhancement	0.50%	0.00%	0.00%
First Year Equity Yield	N/A	10.00%	10.00%

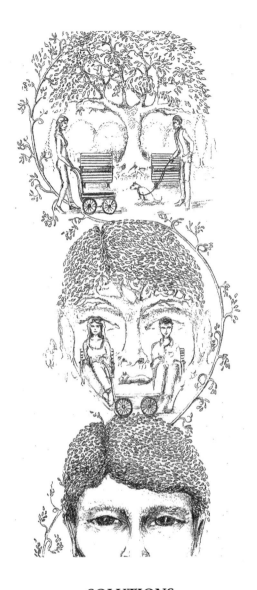

SOLUTIONS

Many of us get boxed into linear thinking about ways to continue the game of providing decent affordable housing. Sometimes different perceptions can come together to make a great solution although they are from unknown sources.

CAPITAL SOLUTIONS

Pool Replacement Reserves Across Portfolio

DISCUSSION: This is the practice of "robbing Peter to pay Paul". With a relatively large portfolio, you may be able to apply the excess reserves from one project to the current needs of another. This is generally not true for syndicated projects, but in most other types of financing, this pooling of reserves has the tendency to extend the life as long as one or two of the properties has healthy reserves that can head off catastrophe and extend the roofing life of the property without reserves.

PROS: The big advantage is that it can see you through a short, 5 or 6-year period when you know the cash is going to be low through to your next refinancing or recapitalization.

CONS: The entire portfolio fails simultaneously when funds evaporate. The bad part about this technique is that when you run out of money, you run out of money for all of the projects on exactly the same day. In a sense, you can bankrupt the entire portfolio creating a huge demand for capital simultaneously.

BEST USE: As a short-term plan to see you through to a known refinance state.

Add Alternative Income

DISCUSSION: Property owners have been very creative and inventive in looking at methods to pump up their overall income. Some have included cell owner leases on their roofs. Others have charged parking fees both for residents and nonresidents. Other groups have been required to charge fees for various services.

PROS: It is very important to keep your income stream healthy and exceeding your expenses. All of these ideas and others should always be pursued to keep a healthy and well-financed property.

CONS: Following these and other economic options can distract from the primary purpose of creating affordable housing and neighborhood revitalization.

BEST USE: Anywhere. Additional income is always appreciated,

Raise Rent

DISCUSSION: The simplest way to meet capital needs is to raise the rents to the point where a sufficient reserve is constantly maintained so that the building can pay for itself. Depending on the building and initial construction, it might involve a per unit/per annum replacement reserve of $2,000 to $3,000 per unit/per year. If you can raise the rents $154 a month, the building will be self-sufficient and will operate ad infinitum.

PROS: It's simple. It means that you are self-sufficient and that you don't have to go back to lenders in the future. If you can make it past that first mortgage period, you will begin to be able to put the entire mortgage payment into the capital reserve fund.

CONS: As affordable housing providers, sometimes increased rents conflict directly with our mission to house lower-income individuals and families.

BEST USE: Healthy real estate markets with relatively high median incomes.

Appeal Your Property Tax

DISCUSSION: Barry Mankowitz, the smartest real estate manager/ operator I've ever met, suggested that appealing your tax rate is the most effective way to maintain reasonable operating costs. All jurisdictions have a process. Initially you may need to consult a lawyer to mentor you in the process, but in the long run, since you'll be doing this annually for the next 20 years, it should become an owner/staff function.

PROS: It is one of the easiest ways to keep the expense curve from shooting down the income stream.

CONS: Requires time. The applications can run from very simple to requiring significant proof of limited income and other financial factors upon which to base a valid tax rate.

BEST USE: Anywhere. All nonprofits that pay taxes should appeal their assessments annually.

Fund Raise

DISCUSSION: In this model you suggest that neither the banking industry nor the property is capable of recapitalizing the project. You approach the fundraising team and say, "We're going to need $300,000 in 4 years. Start a capital improvement fundraising plan so we'll have the money then."

PROS: This doesn't create a debt on the housing and tenants who live there. It separates the housing from the cost of the housing.

CONS: You have to have a really good fundraising team to raise your capital needs. Also, you may be using a good deal of it for operating support.

BEST USE:	Sympathetic clients, for example, homeless shelters, battered spouses, drug rehabilitation and other specialized populations who are especially to sympathetic donors.

Diet: Cannibalize Units/Close Down Sections Of Building

DISCUSSION:	In this scenario you try to use as little energy as possible while maintaining as many services. When the most distressed units go vacant, you would cannibalize them to use the parts for other more marketable units and permanently close down the space. Other options are to close off entire staircases and secure buildings in order to eliminate any operating costs.
PROS:	Requires no additional cash; takes the least desirable units out of service; provides an option when there are absolutely no additional funds.
CONS:	Following this starvation diet, eventually all of the units become unrentable. The mortgage can't be paid. The process is slowed down but the problem isn't really addressed.
BEST USE:	Soft real estate markets where 10% to 20% vacancy has become common as a delaying tactic until additional refinancing or market conditions improve.

Refinance: The Normal System: Resyndicate

DISCUSSION:	In this scenario you either refinance the property with housing bonds or resyndicate with tax credits. The normal cycle of real estate is that every 30 to 50 years it gets substantially renovated or torn down and the land gets reused. If you look back historically, it is not unusual in 40 year cycles to pay twice as much as was initially required to do exactly the same work.

PROS: You can get everything done. It is the best way to get serious amounts of cash back into the structure.

CONS: It takes a lot of lead time, 2 to 3 years of significant planning. If the units are occupied, it may involve relocation.

BEST USE: Anywhere with significant planning and preparation as long as the property still has value.

Sell—At Market or to Another Nonprofit

DISCUSSION: The idea here is that you can sell property, both appreciated and depreciated. Appreciated property may make funds to help sustain the organization and/or other performing units. Depreciated property can be sold to get a barrel off of your back.

PROS: Sometimes older property can generate a considerable amount of profit. In the short term, it eliminates the management task from the properties. If the properties have appreciated greatly, it may be possible to create more units in a different location.

CONS: If your mission was perpetual affordability for rental units, depending on who the purchaser is, this may go against your stated mission or there are times when it may promote it.

BEST USE: Highly appreciated property (for instance, a project purchased for $500,000 that can be sold for $5,000,000) and the funds reinvested in either the current portfolio or new units is the best use. At the other extreme, property that is a drag on the cash flow and management capacities of the sponsor may need to be jettisoned to allow the organization to operate at its best.

Renegotiate Current Loan

DISCUSSION: In this option, you stop paying the mortgage payments and turn to the lender to renegotiate the loan to a level that the property can afford while completing deferred improvements.

PROS: It gets all the parties to identify the issues. If the negotiation is successful, it can save the project.

CONS: This approach may eventually end up in foreclosure by the lender if they do not trust that the current sponsor is capable of turning the property around. It almost always results in pretty extreme damage to the partnership relationship and the overall reputation of the sponsor.

BEST USE: To triage a portfolio. When all the other options haven't played out, it is essential that you move to protect the remaining portfolio.

How Can the HOME PJ Help When a Property Faces Difficulty?

Owners should notify and involve the PJ when initial efforts to address problems in the property are not effective. It is in the PJ's interest to work with owners to keep HOME-assisted properties viable and operational. In order to maintain affordable housing stock in the jurisdiction and avoid repayment of HOME funds to HUD, consider the following:

Invest additional funds in the property. PJs are not permitted to reinvest additional HOME funds in a property during the period of affordability, after the initial 12 months after project completion. PJs may request a waiver of this requirement from HUD once all other options have been pursued.

Charge higher rents, if possible. If the property is not charging rents up to the maximum High and Low HOME Rents, the owner and PJ should evaluate whether increasing rents is a viable option, given the neighborhood market rents and targeted tenant population. If the owner is able to demonstrate to the PJ that the HOME rents are not sufficient to cover operating costs, the PJ may request an exception to the rent limits from HUD. Exception rents are approved in very limited circumstances, when HUD determines that all other options have been exhausted. HUD cannot waive income targeting requirements, as they are statutory.

Re-designate assisted units as non-assisted and increase rents accordingly. This option is available only in properties where the PJ initially designated a *higher* number of HOME-assisted units than the minimum number required by HUD. This change requires an amendment to the written agreement between the owner and the PJ. The PJ must notify HUD.

Restructure the financing through refinancing the property or re-amortizing the loan(s) on the property to lower mortgage payments.

Foreclose on the property if the PJ is a lender and the owner defaults on loan payments. If there are other lien holders, the PJ will need to negotiate the terms of the foreclosure and develop an appropriate workout plan.

—The PJ's rights to take action before the property goes into foreclosure or is transferred in lieu of foreclosure should be specified in the PJ's written agreement with the owner.

—In the event of foreclosure, the PJ is responsible for ensuring that the property remains HOME-compliant. If it is not, the PJ must repay to HUD the outstanding HOME loan balance or grant amount.

—Sell or transfer the property.

—If the property is transferred to a new owner, and the new owner enters into a written agreement subjecting the property to the remaining HOME affordability requirements, HUD considers the affordability requirements satisfied. However, this may not absolve the original owner of the obligation to repay the HOME assistance to the PJ. This decision is at the PJ's discretion.

EXAMPLE PRESERVATION FINANCING SOURCES—CONNECTICUT
2013

SOURCES	MECHANISMS	DESCRIPTION	NOTES
PRIVATE LENDERS			
Lending Institutions: Savings & Loan Banks Commercial Banks Mutual Savings Banks Mortgage Companies e.g. J.P. Morgan Chase	- Market interest loans - Market underwriting - $1 billion available	• Traditional source of mortgage and construction loans. • Low and moderate income lending encouraged by Community Reinvestment Act and Federal Housing Finance Board Affordable Housing Program and Community Investment Program.	
Bank Community Development Corporations		• Bank subsidiaries that initiate, develop and finance community rehab projects. • Bank CDCs act as direct developers of affordable housing.	
Linked Deposits		• Individual corporation, organization or institutional investor places funds in a bank of which all or a portion of the total amount is lent for community development on terms agreed to in advance.	
BENEVOLENT AND CHARITABLE LENDING			
Mercy Loan Fund CDFI	- Refinance renovation $500,000 to $4 million	• To nonprofit and affordable housing; rate 6%, DCR 1.2; 70% LTV	
Preservation of Affordable Housing (POAH)	- Restructure ownership		

SOURCES	MECHANISMS	DESCRIPTION	NOTES
FEDERAL HOUSING PROGRAMS			
HOME	- Grants - Loans - Equity/interest subsidies		
Rehabilitation Loans	- Low interest loans	• Used for repairs and related rehab expenses • May not exceed $33,500 per dwelling unit • Loans are repayable over 20 years at 3% interest rate	
USDA Rural Development	- Section 515 preservation revolving loan	• Flexible term for national competition for $19 million total; limited to 515, 514, 516 projects	
Community Development Block Grant (CDBG)	- Annual grant - Loans	• Flexible source of funding because interest rates and repayment terms can be structured appropriately for various target groups	
HUD Multifamily Preservation Loan Program	- 1% interest used in conjunction with bond financing	• Facilitate workouts with HUD mortgagers, rehab, properties with Section 8 priority	
Low Income Tax Credit	- Tax credit	• May help Section 202 and 236 the second time around	
Section 202 Tools	- Prepay, refinance	• Prepayment, refinancing, subordinations, renewal of contracts	

SOURCES	MECHANISMS	DESCRIPTION	NOTES
FEDERAL HOUSING PROGRAMS			
FHA Mortgage Insurance 223(F) or 221(d)4	- Mortgage insurance of private funds	• Substantial rehab can combine with LIHTC	
FHA Mortgage 236 or 221(d)3	- Interest reduction - Deferred repayment	• Programs to aid properties reaching their expiration dates	
STATE HOUSING PROGRAMS			
Housing Development Fund	- Interest-free seed money - Loans	• Loans generally cover front end costs	
Housing Trust Fund	- Grants - Loans	• Government established fund financed from alternative sources—earmarked for low and moderate income housing • Funded from ongoing revenue sources—fixed endowments, revenue streams (eg. Escrow accounts, interest on funds, taxes, fees	
Other State Programs	- Grants - Loans - Tax credits	• Many states also set up other housing programs using federal or state monies.	
CHFA CNA Loan	- Capital needs funding	• Last resort source	
CHFA Bond Financing	- Refinance renovation	• Threshold review required to qualify	
SOURCES	**MECHANISMS**	**DESCRIPTION**	**NOTES**

LOCAL HOUSING PROGRAMS

Linkage Programs	- Grants - Loans	• For-profit developers contribute units or money because of a municipal ordinance or to gain special development rights (eg. building height or unit density bonuses)				
Property Tax Abatements or Exemptions						
Other Local Programs	- Grants - Loans - Tax credits	• Many communities have other program using federal or state monies.	Local Community Development Agency			
City Programs e.g. Housing Preservation Loan Fund (Hartford)	- 4% loans - 10 year term	• Max $10,000 per unit; builder must carry				

SOURCES	MECHANISMS	DESCRIPTION	NOTES
INTERMEDIARIES			
HAC Preservation Loan	- Refinancing and rehab	• Requires capital needs assessment for 515 properties	

Chapter 10

ASSET MANAGEMENT HANDBOOK

FOR MORE INFORMATION

Theme: One book and 40 hours is just the beginning. Keep learning.

Learning Objectives:
- Continue to prepare for:
  — Annual capital plans
  — Refinancing
  — Sale/merger

Essential Vocabulary:
— Corporate Immortality
— Positive Cash Flow
— Continuous Growth

FINAL WORDS

I've had the opportunity to help build five of the United States largest and most successful nonprofit organizations.

10 TECHNIQUES TO ENSURE CORPORATE IMMORTALITY

1. Build a highly efficient and productive real estate development system.

2. Feed the system 3 to 4 projects in development/predevelopment with the goal of completing 1 project per year for the next 20 years.

3. Underwrite to receive the maximum developer's fee at closing of stabilized rents.

4. Underwrite so that there is positive cash flow for the first 17 years. (See following spreadsheet)

5. Hire aggressive, "go-getter," productive, workaholic staff.

6. Build a helpful, mentoring, powerful board and use 3 consultants.

7. Do a project every other year whose single goal is to build the company's annuity.

8. Never grant funds. Always allow it to be repaid upon sale or conveyance in order to maximize your proceeds.

9. Aggressively fundraise from nonfederal sources.

10. Think BIG.

Live well and prosper.

DINNER POT

Because the federal, state, and local governments allow you to keep some of your money, socialists claim you are "on the dole." This is complete nonsense. Either you put money into the pot or you take money out of the pot. Your job is to keep those two actions in balance, preferably building up very positive cash flows and assets during the healthy times. During periods of great growth, nonprofits should create reserves to expend in the well-established troughs, depressions, and slow growth time periods that are inevitable in our economic system.

ONE SUCCESSFUL CDC'S 2012 PROPERTY CASH FLOW DISTRIBUTIONS

Property	Quarterly Distr	Dev Fee	Co Mgmt Fee	Inc Mgmt Fee	Cash Flow	Totals
A		$31,389.00				$31,389.00
B				$6,631.92		$6,631.92
C		$15,593.40				$15,593.40
D		$4,173.00				$4,173.00
E	$17,762.00	$4,326.00				$22,088.00
F						$ -
G		$47,718.00				$47,718.00
H		$3,624.42	$10,016.00			$13,640.42
I		$8,332.01				$8,332.01
J		$50,682.88			$7,840.11	$58,522.99
K			$4,680.50			$4,680.50
L		$25,254.00				$25,254.00
M	$43,102.00				$3,783.00	$46,885.00
N				$14,233.12		$14,233.12
Total	$60,864.00	$191,092.71	$14,696.50	$20,865.04	$11,623.11	$299,141.36
Cash Flow from Shared Properties			$108,158.96			
Cash Flow from Solely Owned Properties			$190,982.40			
TOTAL			$299,141.36			

This is one CDC's real portfolio. Does your 14-property portfolio return $300,000 in 5 different flavors of return? Why Not?

ADDITIONAL TRAINING

R.M. Santucci, Urban Renovation Consultants, Inc.; P.O. Box 799, Beaufort, NC 28516; 252-728-6924; urcusa@mac.com

Asset Management Practicum: Preserving for the Next Generation

The most progressive and innovative sponsors have enthusiastically endorsed the Asset Management Practicum. In 4, 5 or 6 sessions over 4 to 5 months, the participants are mentored through a process to evaluate their portfolios, establish benchmarks, investigate operating issues and create a long-term plan for portfolio success.

Practicum Application. The training team collects background information on the group, the personnel and at least one property to be used as a case study. This allows the facilitator and the local technical assistance providers to become much more informed about their protégés.

A 4-Session Series with Technical Assistance Between Each Session:

Capital Needs & Portfolio Inspection: Here we figure out how many components you have, how old they are, how long they are going to last and help each participant come up with a very thorough, 30-year capital needs assessment for their individual case study.

Capital Needs—Financial Projections & Narrative: We match up capital needs with sources, turning the raw needs assessment data into a plan. We will clean up our initial drafts describing both the case study and our entire portfolio. We start by looking at the portfolios from an asset management perspective and evaluating the operating characteristics from both a risk and a total performance basis.

Operating & Capital Solutions: This session uses local guest speakers to identify likely and practical sources of recapitalizing our long-term needs and potential sources of refinancing entire properties.

Finalize Presentation & Graduation: We put the final touches on a PowerPoint slide show to present our case study and portfolio analysis to our community. The graduation ceremony is semi-formal and is attended by local intermediaries, board members, lending institutions, government entities, all who have an interest in seeing the current portfolio preserved well into the future.

Urban Renovation Consultants, Inc.
Onsite Training Offerings

www.URCUSA.com

Professional Real Estate & Construction Management Training

Urban Renovation Consultants, Inc. • Robert M. Santucci • Senior Consultant
P.O. Box 799 • Beaufort, N.C. 28516
252-728-6924 (phone) • 252-728-7128 (fax) • urcusa@mac.com
(email)

Training for Tomorrow—Today
May 17, 2013

WHY URC?

We Wrote the Book—Every Time—For You.

All of our courses are: developed by our staff, peer reviewed, and tested in the field. We have a lot of imitators. Great flattery, but why not buy the original? The facilitators are exciting communicators who will engage you with the most interesting days you've ever spent at a desk.

Your Participants Are Fulfilled.

"It's the best housing training course I have ever been to . . . the interaction with participants is very constructive." St. Louis County Office of C.D.

"Bob Santucci provided a wealth of knowledge . . . great mix of content and interaction . . . a 'put at ease' trainer." Barre Vermont N.H.S.

"Outstanding . . . I can go back to my job and immediately begin application." Druid Heights CDC, Baltimore Maryland

You Are in Outstanding Company.

Enterprise Communities
Neighborhood Reinvestment
Corporation
Local Initiative Support Corporation
Harvard, Yale, Rutgers, Portland State
ICF Consulting
HUD, EPA, TDA Inc.
And 110 Jurisdictions

> *"The URC approach to teaching, coaching and technical assistance is the best in the field."*
>
> Kent Buhl
> Sr. Information Specialist
> Enterprise Communities

A+ Quality and Content

You receive essential job-enhancing information in a fast-paced, one—two—or three-day format that respects your time. Our balanced courses reinforce key information for immediate use. Participant materials follow up with complex details including a USB with toolkits of policies, procedures, and documents.

URC COURSE CATALOG
ADULT REAL ESTATE TRAINING—2013

After 22,000 satisfied customers (and six very upset participants), Urban Renovation Consultants, Inc. maintains a solid reputation as an effective, hands-on, training organization. We provide onsite training through intermediaries, government agencies, housing authorities, and associations on a wholesale basis. Our real estate courses fall into four categories:

The Sustainable Building Series presents healthy, accessible, and green building options without breaking the bank. We never left the 1960's "organic/build responsible" field. In the 1970's we owned an energy management firm so we can share the best ways to minimize your: initial, operating and lifecycle costs.

The Production Management Offerings focuses on the skills, procedures, and tools used by efficient production managers. The construction offerings are packaged in three tracks: The Rehab Specialist Series, The Owner's Representative Series, and the Advanced Construction Management series.

Program Design Series informs chief executive officers, senior project managers, board members, and funders responsible for planning, managing, and designing the programs that will lead to the housing of all America.

Custom Offerings. All courses can be customized to reflect the requirements of a single state, a specific program, or a single funding source. Our clients have a wide range, from Harvard's Graduate School of Design to local Coop Boards of Directors. We have presented for the United Nations, Australian Territories, and Caribbean Islands. Our style is outspoken, direct, and above all practical.

We provide your team with proven success tools. Contact us for a proposal on your training needs, refer us to your colleagues, or consider a technical assistance follow-up to your training.

URC TRAINING OFFERS . . .

Experienced and Enjoyable Trainers. Our trainers have received awards of training excellence. The facilitators are masters of live instruction, a dynamic mixture of education and entertainment. Each senior trainer has at least 25 years in the field. If we haven't done it, we don't offer it. Each has completed at least 200 single-family renovations and 500 multi-family rentals. Our senior trainers have written on average 4 books and have published over 80 articles in 25 publications. Check out *www.affordablebusinessplanning.com*.

They are the best of two worlds—real, hands-on developers who have also mastered the craft of adult training. Come see for yourself. They will change your concept of the benefits and advantages of classroom instruction.

Accelerated Learning Techniques. Our trainings are dynamic. Sessions are based in the proven theories of high performance education. Our methods include: team activities, readings, role plays, case studies, and process building. National training organizations know the playing field and they hire URC to train their trainers.

Networking Opportunities. Participants expect to network and share successful concepts with peers. Our trainings promote cooperation to speed understanding. Team exercises facilitate networking and cross fertilization of ideas to solve mutual issues.

Resource Manual. Participants receive 60 pages per day of professionally designed materials. Our manuals are distilled from thousands of experiences and hundreds of articles. These manuals track the training and provide a back home reference guide. They include practice sheets, case studies, examples, and instructional narrative.

For More Information. We recommend Internet sites, books, and periodicals. Education is never complete. We direct you to the materials we found most beneficial. And how do we know? Because our staff absorbs materials: 10 monthly publications; 40 books in a slow year, 100 in a good one. No novels, no fiction. We even predigest the Federal Register so you don't have to.

USB Toolkits. All courses include a take home bonus. Electronic copies of procedures manuals, spreadsheets, and document packets for at home customization. Many courses are based on books authored by our senior trainers who will share copies. In the Business Planning, Asset Management, and other practicums, a USB drive is provided containing multiple examples, templates, spreadsheet options, and huge replacement reserve calculation spreadsheets with multiple options.

OWNER'S REPRESENTATIVE SERIES

MULTIFAMILY PROJECT MANAGEMENT

This series examines larger projects involving architects, engineers, site planners and general contractors. These courses have been the backbone of both the NeighborWorks® Certification and the Enterprise Communities initial training for multifamily construction.

- Design Development for Owner's Representatives
- Design Review for Project Managers
- Multifamily Construction Management
- Cost Reduction in Property
- Asset Management
- Capital Reserves Overview: Keeping Buildings Operating

Design Development for Owner's Representatives: **2 Day**

Evaluate the 5 traditional models of production and learn a system for qualifying and selecting architects and engineers. Use computer templates and exercises to clarify design standards for a specific project. Review AIA contracts and the modifications to them that empower the owner. First in a series of three courses in the recommended program of study for owner's representatives.

* **Goal:** Establish systems to select and oversee high quality design professionals using AIA formats and contracts.

* **Audience:** Owner's representatives, construction managers, project managers, development directors

* **Topics Learned:** RFP/RFQ systems, due diligence reviews, planning & zoning responsibilities, AIA contract documents, using the Design Advisor tool

* **USB Bonus:** Design Advisor Tool, RFQ 12 Step System with 9 template documents, AIA document revisions

Design Review for Owner's Representatives: **1 Day**

Keeping the design process on time and building costs within the budget is a project manager's primary task. Blueprint review is practiced. Learn ways to manage the relationship between the owner and the architect during the evolving design process, and identify cost-saving measures you can use back home.

* **Goal:** Investigate tools & procedures to evaluate, modify and communicate revisions to architectural drawings.

* **Audience:** Owner's representatives, construction managers, project managers, development directors

* **Topics Learned:** Review drawing symbols & terms, value engineering, CSI format design program, design review systems

* **USB Bonus:** Multifamily Programming Guide

Multifamily Construction Management: **2 Day**

Examine AIA protocols for field supervision, payment systems and job closeout. Review the basics of win/win negotiation during construction. Examine the change order process, select techniques to maintain project momentum while retaining control, and learn methods of establishing and enforcing the warranty. The third course in the Owner's Rep Program of Study.

*   **Goal:** Offer methods to maintain job on schedule, under budget and as designed.

*   **Audience:** Owner's representatives, construction managers, project managers

*   **Topics Learned:** Awarding construction contracts, monitoring job progress, win/win negotiation, payment procedures with G702-703, revision documents and job close-out

*   **USB Bonus:** Policy and procedures including 20 document templates

Cost Reduction In Multifamily Property: **2 Day**

The first step is to identify the sources of the problem. Each participant is encouraged to bring an annual operating statement to compare against established benchmarks for property and asset management. You compile ways to operate more efficiently to reduce costs with a special session on green energy conservation techniques. Other times there is just not enough rent to go around. Analyze the most effective ways to increase income. Sometimes the issue is structural and cannot be solved by either short-term operating or income solutions. Investigate long-term solutions that can bring relief to stressed projects.

*   **Goal:** Identify areas of income loss and excessive cost and multiple techniques to address them.

* **Audience:** Property managers, executive directors, asset managers, project managers

* **Topics Learned:** Issue analysis; reduction of operating costs; green and energy savings; increasing income, and long-term solutions

* **USB Bonus**: Operating benchmarks

Asset Management: **2 Day**

Local assessments indicate that 50% of CDC portfolios have serious asset management indicator shortfalls. CDCs need to quantify and assess their situation, make future projections, evaluate alternatives and make strategic short—and long-term plans for their assets.

* **Goal:** By the end of the program participants will:
  * Benchmark portfolio operations
  * Identify physical assessment needs
  * Track and forecast spreadsheets
  * Evaluate opportunities to increase income and reduce expenses
  * Draft action plan addressing long-term viability.

* **Audience:** Owners, property managers, asset managers with portfolios containing at least 30 units and up to 2000 units

* **Topics Learned:** Asset versus property management, benchmarking and risk analysis, CNAs, long-term solutions

* **USB Bonus:** Extensive Excel spreadsheet to computerize capital needs reserves, benchmarking templates

Capital Reserves Overview: Keeping Buildings Operating: **2 Day**

Will we have enough money to replace the roof and the boiler? When will we need to refinance the property? We answer these questions as academics on the first day and field inspectors on the second. Together the activities offer great take-home experience in identifying the reserve needs of your multifamily dwellings.

*   **Goal:** Evaluate your multifamily projects' remaining economic life and your plan to keep the structure alive and healthy into the next century.

*   **Audience:** Asset managers, senior production managers, property managers, underwriters, executive directors

*   **Topics Learned:** 4 ways to calculate a capital reserve, property inspection techniques, remaining life formulas, how to use URC Excel template to project long-term reserves

*   **USB Bonus:** Replacement Reserve Tracking Spreadsheets, life cycle time periods, example replacement reserve reports

CUSTOM TRAININGS/ TECHNICAL ASSISTANCE

All courses can be customized to reflect the requirements of a single state, a specific program, or a single funding source. Our clients have a wide range, from Harvard's Graduate School of Design to local Coop Boards of Directors. We have presented for the United Nations, Australian Territories, and Caribbean Islands. Our style is outspoken, direct, and above all practical.

URC has enjoyed the opportunity to design and facilitate numerous custom training programs. While direct development of materials for a specific audience involves extensive effort, it can quickly solve a current specific problem. If you are training five or more staff in a single subject area, it can be cost-effective to contract for a custom course. Past offerings included:

• Cost Effective Section 3 Compliance
• Double Your Production
• Energy Management in Affordable Housing
• Affordable Design Workshop—Best Values in New Construction
• Cost Versus Value Debate
• Saving Money with Modular Construction
• Risk Assessment Protocols for Lead Risk Assessors
• Why Nonprofits Fail (and what you can do)
• LIHTC Compliance, CNA, and Physical Requirements
• Davis-Bacon Compliance
• Federal Procurement Rules
• Post Flood Mold Remediation

CONTRACT CONSIDERATIONS

How To Sponsor Our Trainings:

Local intermediaries, state and city jurisdictions, associations of CDCs, foundations and grant makers are invited to contact our senior consultant, R.M. Santucci. After a phone consultation, URC will develop a customized proposal to address your specific training requirements.

The traditional lead-time to schedule a single training is 3 months. We often sell out fall months up to 18 months in advance.

Include one of our exciting learning experiences in your long-term planning. Call us today at 252-728-6924. Let us create and deliver a learning experience for your developers.

How about On-Site Technical Assistance?

An efficient way to build and maintain skills is to use a continuum of interventions. Start with a distance review of your current documentation. After an iterative pass or two of review modifications and edits, we select training modules that incorporate these new and improved documents. Then a 1- to 2-day onsite training puts the policy and procedure documents in play. We follow up with support via webinar, phone conference or email correspondence to ensure the activity is implemented efficiently.

URBAN RENOVATION CONSULTANTS, INC.
TRAINING DELIVERY RATES
2009-2013

Off-the-shelf, one, two and three day trainings usually require a day of travel each way, and at least 8 hours of preparation.

You get direct access to experts who have aided hundreds of organizations and know what works.

Let our professional staff travel to your location. It's the most cost effective way to maintain staff skills and keep up with the newest technology.

One Day Overview   **$5,400**

  — plus training materials
  — plus travel expenses
   $150 per participant day*

Two Day Course   **$6,900**

  — plus training materials
  — plus travel expenses
   $90 per participant day*

Four or Five Day "Institute"   **$10,400**

  — plus training materials
  — plus travel expenses
   *$57 per participant day for comprehensive, on-site training Your Best Buy

*Assumes 36 participants

Made in the USA
Columbia, SC
28 August 2023

22225352R00126